Gristle

From Factory Farms to Food Safety

(Thinking Twice About the Meat We Eat)

Co-edited by Moby with Miyun Park

THE NEW PRESS

NEW YORK
LONDON

This collection would not have come to life without Paul Petersan, Sara Shields, Gowri Koneswaran, Bowen Cho, and Benjamin Davidow. Thank you. And thanks, again, to our incredible contributors . . . and to each of you for wanting to seek out more information on how we can transform animal agriculture for the betterment of workers, our environment, communities, health, the hungry, the poor, and the animals themselves.

Requests for permission to reproduce selections from this book should be mailed to:
Permissions Department, The New Press, 38 Greene Street, New York, NY 10013.

Published in the United States by The New Press, New York, 2010
Distributed by Perseus Distribution

LIBRARY OF CONGRESS CATALOGING-IN-PUBLICATION DATA
Gristle : from factory farms to food safety (thinking twice about
the meat we eat) / co-edited by Moby with Miyun Park.
p. cm.
ISBN 978-1-59558-191-4 (pb)
1. Meat. 2. Food of animal origin. 3. Factory farms. I. Moby. II. Park, Miyun.
TX371.G75 2010
641.3'6—dc22   2009046697

The New Press was established in 1990 as a not-for-profit alternative to the large,
commercial publishing houses currently dominating the book publishing industry.
The New Press operates in the public interest rather than for private gain, and
is committed to publishing, in innovative ways, works of educational, cultural,
and community value that are often deemed insufficiently profitable.

www.thenewpress.com

Composition by dix!
This book was set in MetaPlus

Printed in the United States of America

2 4 6 8 10 9 7 5 3 1

Contents

Introduction

Moby

In some ways I wish that I had more objectivity regarding the subject of this book. But alas, I have an agenda. I'm a vegan and animal protection advocate. (This almost sounds as if I'm at a meeting of Vegans Anonymous: "Hi, my name's Moby, and I'm a vegan.") My agenda is simple: to one day be the first democratically elected dictator of the world and its satellite, the moon.

Oops. That's a different agenda. My agenda as regards animals and animal welfare is also simple: to end animal suffering. My agenda had its nascence when I was quite young and I first heard the golden rule: "Do unto others as you'd have them do unto you." That's the golden rule, right? When I was young, this made a lot of sense to me in an uncluttered and beautifully self-evident way.

But it then begged a follow-up question: who are these "others" referred to in the golden rule? Should this golden rule only apply to me and my family? Should it extend to friends? Strangers? And what about animals? To my young mind, it seemed inconceivable that I would extend the golden rule to strangers, but not to the animals in my house (three pet rats, two dogs, three cats, and a cranky iguana).

I loved the animals in my house, so I decided that I should extend the golden rule to them. Which then begged another follow-up question: If I don't want the animals in my house to suffer,

Moby is one of the world's most critically acclaimed and commercially successful musicians. Known for his political and social activism, he has been a vegan for more than twenty years.

well, then, what about the animals who don't live in my house? Shouldn't the golden rule apply to them as well? So, at an early age, I decided that the golden rule should probably extend to all animals who seem to have the capacity to suffer.

Years later, when I was a pretentious philosophy student, I read about Pascal's wager. Pascal, a French philosopher, basically posited that it made more logical sense to "bet" on God's existence than to "bet" on God's nonexistence (kind of a shaky theological premise, but an interesting logical position).

I took the logic of this and applied it to my extension of the golden rule to humans and animals. I decided that it's probably a better "bet" to extend compassion as far and wide as possible, as opposed to restricting the lengths to which I was willing to extend compassion.

Later I was able to expand upon my golden rule extension, and I came up with a happy little logical-sounding catchphrase to justify my veganism and animal protection advocacy: Death is unavoidable, but suffering is avoidable. Just as I hope to avoid unnecessary suffering in my life, I can assume that all beings capable of suffering also hope to avoid it; therefore, we should do our best to prevent suffering.

As I got further into veganism and the animal protection movement, I found that my decision to be an animal advocate was also supported by a lot of nonanimal welfare criteria.

That's what this book is about, the rarely publicized ramifications of industrialized farmed animal production and meat, egg, and milk consumption on the environment, human health, communities, workers, taxpayers, zoonotic diseases, global warming, global hunger, and, of course, the animals themselves.

There are huge and egregiously well-financed interests who want to keep the truth of animal production hidden. (Although, who knows, maybe some of these egregiously well-financed interests are currently sitting in the corporate bathroom reading this introduction. If so: hi, thanks for reading.)

We don't have their money, but we have two very powerful things: naiveté and the truth. Hopefully, if enough people find out about the hidden ramifications of industrialized farmed animal production, we'll eventually see a shift away from supporting these destructive industries, which would lead to a healthier, cleaner, and more humane world. That's my agenda. Hopefully, it'll all make more sense after you read the book.

Thanks,
Moby
New York City, 2009

"If we want a healthier diet, and I say this as a livestock producer, we must move to a diet less centered on animal products. Moving away from grain-fattened livestock will reduce corn and soy acreage, making more land available for staple food crops, rangeland and forests."[1]

—Jim Goodman, W.K. Kellogg Food and Society Policy Fellow and organic beef and dairy farmer

1

Health

Brendan Brazier

Unlike most other fifteen-year-olds in Vancouver, my priorities didn't revolve around football games against high school rivals, dating, or who would win the 1990 Stanley Cup. But, like most kids my age, I was a bit obstinate and a bit reluctant not to question authority.

So, as a serious, young athlete who already knew that I wanted to compete as a professional Ironman triathlete, I found the pro-meat mantra of my coach and trainers a little hard to swallow.

An Ironman triathlon consists of a 3.2-mile swim, a 112-mile bike ride, and a 26.2-mile marathon. I didn't need a coach to tell me that I had a huge amount of training ahead of me. Given how much time I would need to invest in preparing my body for professional competition, I knew that, to get a head start, I needed the most effective training program possible. Since imitation can be the highest form of flattery, I looked at the training programs of some of the top professional Ironman triathletes in the world, with the plan of mimicking their routine. To see what elevated the best from the rest, I also looked at the training regimens of those with respectable,

Brendan Brazier, two-time Canadian 50km Ultra Marathon Champion, raced Ironman triathlons professionally for seven years before becoming a bestselling author on performance nutrition and the creator of Vega, an award-winning line of whole food nutritional products.

yet average, performance. What I found surprised me: the average athlete's program differed very little from the elite's.

If training discrepancies were minimal and natural talent can only get you so far so fast, what caused some athletes to pull out ahead of the pack?

The most significant difference I found between the upper echelon of elites and the moderately performing athletes had nothing to do with training; it was all about recovery. Breakthrough performances are hinged on the rate at which the body recovers from physical training—which makes sense. Training isn't much more than breaking down muscle tissue, so it stands to reason that the athletes who can restore theirs the quickest will have the advantage by being able to schedule more workouts closer together. Over just a few short months, that extra training will translate into a significant performance gain. Realizing this, recovery became my focus.

As surprised as I was to discover that there were few differences in training routines between the best and the average athlete, I was even more so when I learned that diet has the single greatest impact on recovery: food choices can account for up to 80 percent of the total recovery process. If cleaning up my diet was a principal component to becoming a professional athlete, as I speculated it might be, I needed to learn more. With this newfound appreciation for diet, I decided to take mine more seriously and, for the first time, developed an increasingly growing interest in health and nutrition.

In those early years, I experimented with many different nutritional philosophies, ticking them off as I methodically continued my search for the diet that would give me the results I was looking for. At long last, I tried a purely plant-based diet. Right from the outset, my meat-, egg-, and dairy-free diet was unexpectedly met with extraordinary resistance by friends, coaches, and train-

ingestion question

harvard school of public health:
"eating a plant-based diet is healthiest."*
really, though, what can meat, eggs, and dairy do to me?

chicken

chickens are the most common cause of food poisoning in the home, sickening millions annually. more than 90% of chicken carcass pieces tested at retail are contaminated with *e. coli* and *campylobacter* from fecal matter. one bout of *campylobacter* can lead to lifelong irritable bowel syndrome.

fish

the mercury exposure of eating a single daily serving of tuna is the equivalent to having 49 mercury-containing amalgam fillings in your mouth.

beef

mad cow disease (bovine spongiform encephalopathy) can cause an invariably fatal disease decades after eating beef. the pathogens can't be cooked out, even surviving incineration at temperatures hot enough to melt lead.

pork

the leading cause of seizures in the world is the brain parasite *taenia solium*, a tapeworm found in pork.

eggs

salmonella-infected eggs cause a foodborne epidemic every year in the united states, sickening more than 100,000 annually. one bout of *salmonella* can leave a lifetime of chronic arthritis. and eating just one egg a day was linked to significantly higher all-cause mortality in the harvard physicians' health study (studying about 20,000 physicians for 20 years), compared with eating oatmeal each morning, which may extend life.

dairy

consumption of dairy products has been so strongly linked to acne that the international academy of cosmetic dermatology published a commentary in its journal *clinics in dermatology* calling for a "no dairy diet." dairy has also been recently linked to twice the risk of heart disease in the harvard nurses' health study, triple the risk of colorectal cancer, and more testicular cancer, prostate cancer, and parkinson's disease.

ers. They all seemed closed to the possibility that a plant-based diet could support the high physical demands of professional Ironman training and racing, and I found their adamant stance intriguing. They assumed that a diet free of animal products was either too low in protein, iron, and calcium or deficient in vitamin B12 and omega-3 fatty acids.

As only a stubborn teenager can, I set out to prove them wrong—and succeeded. I completed my first triathlon in 1993 as a high school competitor. In 1998, at 23, I began my professional career, going on to place eighth in Ironman Utah and third in the National Long-Course Triathlon Championships, and twice winning the Canadian National 50km Ultra Marathon Championships.

Throughout my research, training, dietary experimentation, and competition, I've benefited enormously on a professional level from adopting a diet free of meat, eggs, and dairy products, while, unknowingly, improving my overall health and protecting myself from the many diet-related diseases and disorders that have become commonplace in North America.

According to estimates published in the prestigious peer-reviewed journal *Preventive Medicine*, meat consumption accounts for up to two-thirds of the high blood pressure cases in the United States, about one-quarter of the heart disease cases, maybe 40 percent of certain cancer cases, one-third of the diabetes cases, up to three-quarters of all gallbladder operations, most of the food poisoning cases, and half the obesity cases.

Those who eat meat are twice as likely to become hospitalized, twice as likely to have to be on medications, and more likely to need emergency diagnostic procedures and emergency surgery than vegetarians. And, after the numbers are crunched, the health care costs of meat are astronomical, approaching perhaps $60 billion, comparable with the costs of smoking.

Consumption of animal products has not only elevated our

antibiotics
chickens, egg-laying hens,
pigs, farmed fish
cattle (beef)
cows (milk)
calves (veal)

slaughter waste
**(including blood, fat,
and bonemeal)**
chickens, egg-laying hens,
pigs, farmed fish
cattle (beef)
cows (milk)
calves (veal)

animal waste
**(including pig and cattle
waste and poultry litter)**
chickens, egg-laying hens,
pigs, farmed fish
cattle (beef)
cows (milk)
calves (veal)

when we eat
meat, eggs, and milk,
we also ingest what the
farmed animals ingested
on the side
a sampling of approved feed
"ingredients" and drugs
for administering to
farmed animals

arsenic-based drugs
chickens
egg-laying hens
pigs

growth hormones
cattle (beef)
cows (milk)
calves (veal)

antiparasitics
chickens, egg-laying hens,
pigs, farmed fish
cattle (beef)
cows (milk)
calves (veal)

risks for myriad disorders, it has jeopardized our ability to read-
ily overcome illnesses that could once be treated effectively. As
animal production has become increasingly industrialized over
the decades, factory farming has relied more on dosing farmed
animals with growth promotants and subtherapeutic antibiotics,
which have also taken a toll on human health. In fact, this dangerous practice of feeding medically important antibiotics to factory-

> **Reported an article in *Ecological Economics*, "[b]y changing the preferences of people away from meat consumption to more efficient foods like soy, a positive environmental impact can be made worldwide, as well as creating healthier lives and decreasing the impact of health problems on a society."[2]**

farmed pigs, chickens, and other animals—not to treat illness, but to speed their growth and try to prevent disease contraction in the overcrowded, unsanitary conditions customary in today's intensive facilities—led the European Union more than a decade ago to ban the nontreatment use of antibiotics of human importance in farmed animal production. In the United States, however, nearly twenty classes of antimicrobials are approved for farmed animal growth promotion, according to the Centers for Disease Control and Prevention (CDC), including many critically important antibiotics, such as penicillin, tetracycline, and erythromycin. Estimates from the Union of Concerned Scientists reveal that 70 percent of antimicrobials used in the United States are fed to farmed animals for nontherapeutic purposes. Aquatic farmed animals, too, are fed antibiotics. The U.S. fish farming industry consumes a shocking 50,000 pounds of the drugs in a single year.

What does this mean for our health? Antibiotic-resistant bacteria.

It's scary to consider and even scarier to realize it's a reality: indiscriminate use of antibiotics in today's factory farming systems has allowed bacteria to become more resistant to the antibiotics used to treat us when we're ill. Studies have shown that antibiotic-resistant bacteria—and antibiotics themselves—can be found in

q. which is cleaner?
the kitchen sink or the toilet?

a. the toilet

q. really?

a. really. university of arizona researchers found **more fecal bacteria in the kitchen—on sponges, dish towels, and the sink drain—than they found swabbing the toilet.** even after washing everything with bleach not once, but twice, **in a house with omnivores, it is safer to lick the rim of their toilet seat than the kitchen countertop...because people aren't preparing chickens in the toilet.**

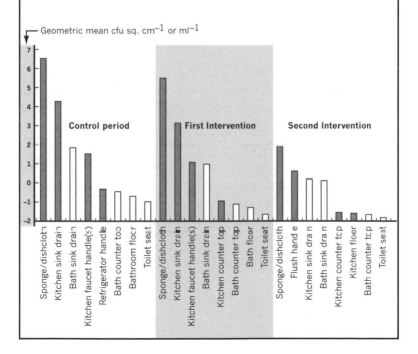

Geometric mean cfu sq. cm^{-1} or ml^{-1}

Control period   First Intervention   Second Intervention

> ## Dieticians "can encourage eating that is both healthful and conserving of soil, water, and energy by emphasizing plant sources of protein and foods that have been produced with fewer agricultural inputs."[3]
>
> —American Dietetic Association, the world's largest association of food and nutrition professionals

the air, water, and soil around facilities, as well as on meat, and we can be exposed through infected animal products and water supplies contaminated by farmed animal waste.

The world's leading medical, agricultural, and veterinary authorities—the World Health Organization, the Food and Agriculture Organization of the United Nations, and the World Organization for Animal Health, respectively—have concluded that animal agribusiness's overuse of antibiotics is, indeed, contributing to human health problems. Add to that the many negative health impacts of diets laden with meat, eggs, and milk (particularly from factory farms), and plant-based diets should look even more attractive, even solely from a personal health perspective.

And nutritionists agree. Vegetarian diets, according to the American Dietetic Association, "are healthful, nutritionally adequate, and provide health benefits in the prevention and treatment of certain diseases. Well-planned vegan and other types of vegetarian diets are appropriate for all stages of the life cycle, including during pregnancy, lactation, infancy, childhood, and adolescence. . . . Vegetarians have been reported to have lower body mass indices than nonvegetarians, as well as lower rates of death from ischemic heart disease; vegetarians also show lower blood cholesterol levels; lower blood pressure; and lower rates of hypertension, type 2 diabetes, and prostate and colon cancer."

Whether it's to enhance your athletic performance, to help to reduce your risk of heart disease or your cholesterol, or simply to achieve better health, leaving farmed animals out of your diet is a simple decision with life-long benefits.

"As an unreconstructed carnivore, I am painfully aware how much land and water go into the raising and slaughter of poultry and livestock compared to growing fruits and vegetables, and I also know how much our meat industries contribute to the destruction of the Chesapeake Bay. Every year I hear from vegetarians about the public environmental and private health benefits of giving up meat, and they're right."[4]

—Senator Jamie Raskin, Maryland State Senator, District 20

Reports the Natural Resources Defense Council, "Factory farms, which mass-produce animals in assembly-line fashion, have harmed aquatic life, human health and ecosystems across the nation. As industrial-sized farms stagger under the vast burden of manure they are generating, environmental disasters are inevitable."[5]

2

Environment

Lauren Bush

For those of us who live in suburbs or cities, the idea of living near a farm may conjure a warm image of borrowing cups of sugar from the neighbors, who raise animals in healthy, open-air pastures and are good stewards to the land. In stark contrast, as Robert F. Kennedy Jr. said so eloquently—and startlingly—"the vast majority of America's meat and produce are controlled by a handful of ruthless monopolies that house animals in industrial warehouses where they are treated with unspeakable and unnecessary cruelty. These meat factories destroy family farms and rural communities and produce vast amounts of dangerous pollutants that are contaminating America's most treasured landscapes and waterways."

Hardly good neighbors, today's farmed animal factories are devastating the environment as they inflict unacceptable cruelties on those cows, pigs, chickens, and other animals confined in their intensive facilities. Industrial meat, egg, and milk factories often pollute the water, land, and air of the communities in which they are located. One of the primary causes of rampant factory farm pollution? Manure.

Confining so many animals—thousands, tens of thousands, hundreds of thousands, and even more than one million on some factory farms—exclusively or primarily indoors generates an incredible amount of excrement. Unbelievably, some operations

Lauren Bush is the chief executive officer and co-founder of FEED Projects.

estimated annual production of farmed animal manure and human urine and feces (in tons)

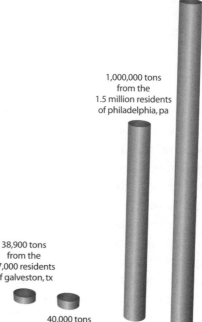

1,600,000 tons
from 800,000 pigs
at 1 pork facility

1,000,000 tons
from the
1.5 million residents
of philadelphia, pa

16,000 tons
from the
24,000 residents
of lake tahoe, ca

17,800 tons
from 700 cattle
at 1 dairy facility

38,900 tons
from the
57,000 residents
of galveston, tx

40,000 tons
from 3,423 cattle
at 1 beef facility

produce as much waste as an entire U.S. city. In fact, according to data from the U.S. Department of Agriculture and the Environmental Protection Agency, animal feeding operations—also known as "AFOs," which are defined by the EPA as facilities that "congregate animals, feed, manure and urine, dead animals, and production operations on a small land area"—produce approximately 500 million tons of manure every year, with concentrated animal feeding operations (CAFOs) generating up to 60 percent of this excrement. To put this in perspective, confined farmed animals produce three times the amount of waste that is produced by all humans in the United States, according to EPA estimates.

On traditional, diversified farms—the ones we imagine with red barns and animals pecking and foraging in the grass—farmers make good use of manure, recycling nutrients to replenish the soil and fertilize crops. They balance the number of animals with the land's ability to absorb the nutrients in their manure. In contrast, factory farms intensively confine too many animals who produce too much waste for the neighboring land to utilize.

Farmed animal waste management problems have gotten even more dire over the past two decades, and the USDA's Natural Resources Conservation Service and the EPA have identified the following key reasons:

- the move toward intensive confinement;

- the steady replacement of small- and medium-sized operations with large confinement operations;

- the continued consolidation of all aspects of production;

- the increase in numbers of confined animals per operation; and

- the spatial concentration of operations in high-production areas.

Simply put, the shift from farms to factories is to blame.

Not surprisingly, water quality concerns are most pronounced in areas of intensive crop cultivation (often for farmed animal feed) and concentrated farmed animal production. Overapplication of manure to land, leaking or overflowing manure cesspools (euphemistically referred to as "lagoons"), and the redepositing of airborne pollutants into waterways have contaminated surface and groundwater with factory farm waste.

The incidences of water pollution are many and occur from coast

According to the U.S. Environmental Protection Agency, the agricultural sector is "the leading contributor to identified water quality impairments in the nation's rivers and streams, lakes, ponds, and reservoirs." In particular, the agency has noted that water quality concerns are most pronounced in areas "where crops are intensively cultivated and where livestock operations are concentrated."[6]

---

to coast. Just a few examples: In 2003, California's Chino basin spent more than $1 million to remove nitrates, which can cause methemoglobinemia, or "blue baby syndrome," from its drinking water, and the source was found to be in the many local dairies and their abundant quantities of manure. From 1995 to 1998, factory farms were responsible for 1,000 "spills" of liquefied manure or other instances of pollution in ten states. When these cesspools leak, they can poison surface and groundwater, and cause massive fish kills. In one incident, more than 20 million gallons of waste spilled from a manure lagoon on a North Carolina pig factory farm into a nearby river, causing a massive fish kill. In 2005, a manure lagoon at an upstate New York dairy farm burst, polluting the nearby Black River with millions of gallons of manure and killing more than 375,000 fish. In Oklahoma, between 2006 and 2007, the EPA levied more than $7 million in fines against companies—primarily factory farms—in the state. Said an EPA director: "If the waste from those facilities . . . [is not] managed properly, you get significant nutrient problems in ground and surface water."

The USDA has found farmed bird production facilities—poultry factory farms—to produce more than half of all of farmed animal

underwater factory farming

fugitive fish: when farmed fish escape, they can harm wild fish populations by competing for food and partners, and spreading diseases and parasites.

feces and feed: wastes and uneaten feed discharged into surrounding waters can cause low- or no-oxygen "dead zones," fish kills, and death of corals and seagrasses.

in the u.s., **more than 10 times more fish (1.6 billion) are farmed than pigs.** off-shore and land-based aquaculture **causes animal suffering, disease, and death, while devastating the environment.** from the pew oceans commission report on its top 5 environmental impacts:

the fish tease: off-shore factory farms can attract predators (herons, cormorants, otters, seals, and others) who can die through accidental entanglement or intentional industry "harassment."

fish pharma: antibiotics, parasiticides, pesticides, hormones, and other chemicals used in aquaculture can negatively impact our health and the health of surrounding ecosystems.

feeding fish fish: farming carnivorous fish means feeding them wild caught fish. one example: 2.5-5 kg of wild-caught fish are needed to feed and produce 1 kg of farmed salmon.

waste-generated excess phosphorous and nearly 65 percent of the excess nitrogen. Chicken waste poses its greatest water pollution risk after it has been applied to land.

Pathogens have also been proven to be problematic for our water supply. Studies have linked farmed animal waste to pathogenic outbreaks of *Campylobacter*, *Salmonella*, *Listeria monocytogenes*, *Helicobacter pylori*, and *E. coli* O157:H7, found in sources of drinking water.

Water isn't the only "natural resource" that is threatened by factory farming. As farmed animal manure decomposes—whether in

spewed from a factory farm

particulate matter, carbon dioxide, ammonia, hydrogen sulfide, nitrous oxide, methane

spewed from a coal power plant

particulate matter, carbon dioxide, ozone, sulfur dioxide, nitrous oxides, mercury

toxic factories

a comparison of air pollutants

an intact cesspool or within the animal factory warehouse itself—noxious levels of gases are spewed into the air, jeopardizing the health of workers, neighbors, and the environment. Particulates from factory farms, including hydrogen sulfide, ammonia, methane, and nitrous oxide, are released into the air and, with them, bacteria, gases, and odors. Hydrogen sulfide, which can build up in underground manure pits, has even been deemed a leading cause of sudden death in the workplace. And, of course, the emission of greenhouse gases from the animal agribusiness industry, as discussed in chapter 5, further illustrates the environmental degradation factory farming causes.

Beyond the inhumane conditions factory-farmed animals endure, these intensive confinement facilities—hardly "farms" at

Reports the Worldwatch Institute, "[A]s environmental science has advanced, it has become apparent that the . . . [animal agriculture sector] is a driving force behind virtually every major category of environmental damage now threatening the human future—deforestation, erosion, fresh water scarcity, air and water pollution, climate change, biodiversity loss, social injustice, the destabilization of communities, and the spread of disease."[7]

all—are truly devastating the environment. Animal agriculture–induced environmental problems have reached such a critical juncture that the Food and Agriculture Organization of the United Nations insists that they be addressed "with urgency." We must shift to more sustainable methods of agriculture, diversify farms, and reduce the numbers of animals raised and killed for meat, egg, and dairy products, and we must do this now.

The way we "farm" animals has become a critical global issue.

To what extent is each of us willing to be conscious of where the food we eat comes from and to take a step away from constraining billions of farmed animals in factories where they are forced to live in unnatural conditions, poisoning water and air, clear-cutting forests, causing loss of biodiversity, and contributing to climate change in the process? The answer to that question has the potential to improve not only the animals' lives but also our own and the life of the planet.

Writes Eric Schlosser in the foreword of *Slaughterhouse Blues: The Meat and Poultry Industry in North America*: "America's current methods of raising livestock and processing meat . . . imposes enormous costs upon society that are not reflected in the price of meat. Much like industrial polluters in the days before environmental laws, today's meatpacking companies are now imposing their business costs on the rest of the nation. . . . [T]he current system needlessly harms workers, consumers, and the environment. It mistreats animals. It brings poverty, drug abuse, and crime to rural communities. When all the social costs are tallied, our cheap meat is much more expensive than we can afford."[8]

3

Taxpayers

John Mackey

I started thinking about food in 1976 while I was living in a housing co-op in Austin, Texas, which is also where I learned how to cook. I eventually became the co-op's food buyer, which started me thinking about how we get the various foods that show up on the shelves of our grocery stores. In 1978, my girlfriend Renee Lawson and I got the entrepreneurial bug, borrowed $45,000 from family and friends, and opened our own small natural foods store. We didn't open with a grand plan—just with the idea of creating a store where you could buy healthy, natural, and organic foods. Two years later, in September 1980, Renee and I partnered with Craig Weller and Mark Skiles, and the first Whole Foods Market opened its doors with a staff of nineteen. It's hard to believe that today, just thirty years later, we now have 280 stores in North America and the United Kingdom, and a staff of 52,000 team members.

Along the way, I've had what I'd call a "food awakening." I realized that the overwhelming majority of the animal-based foods being produced weren't coming to us from small, independent farms where animals grazed in pastures, pecked around barnyards, and felt the sun on their backs. Instead, animal agribusiness operations had largely displaced farms, and the animals had become nothing more than machines.

Farmers became "producers," farmed animals became "food

John Mackey is the chief executive officer and co-founder of Whole Foods Market.

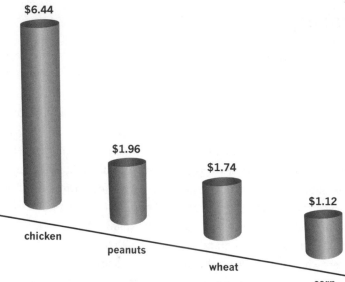

1 person for 1 day: the cost of producing protein, as recommended by the u.s. government

$6.44

$1.96

$1.74

$1.12

chicken

peanuts

wheat

corn

animals," and those "units of production" were intensively confined in smaller and smaller spaces, pushed faster and harder to reach slaughter weight in shorter periods of time and to produce greater amounts of milk, eggs, and offspring than could ever happen naturally.

What is the cost of this transition in farming?

At first glance, it may seem that this "progress" has enabled people to spend more of their income on things other than food, like shoes or travel or housing. But are the total costs of animal-based foods really understood? Do they really reflect all of the inputs and outputs? As you'll read in the other essays in this book, the answer is very definitely *no*, once you factor in all of the tolls industrial animal agriculture exacts.

But if you look only at the prices listed at the market, are people willing to spend more on their groceries if they know they'll be supporting farms that are more sustainable and provide higher animal welfare than today's industrial animal factories?

People ask me this question all the time, and there is no easy answer. It's clear, based on consumer purchasing preference surveys, the expansion of sales from more humane and environmentally responsible farms, and other vehicles, that some people are not only *willing* to spend more for quality products, but are doing so. Of course, others just want the cheapest food possible and maybe have little consciousness about animal welfare when they go shopping. Over the years, these people have told me, "They're *just* chickens, John. They're not humans." My response is always that animals are sentient beings who can experience pain and suffering and therefore are deserving of moral consideration. Fortunately, humanity's consciousness is continuing to evolve to a higher ethical plane, and our goal should be to continue to increase awareness among people who currently couldn't care less about animals or the ways they're raised for meat, eggs, and milk, and the many impacts those irresponsible practices are having.

But, once people are aware, are they willing to pay a premium for products that were produced by more humane (or, conversely, less *inhumane*) practices? There's been a long-term trend toward spending less money on food. At the turn of the twentieth century, we spent about 45 percent of our disposable income in the United States on food. Today, it's about 8 percent. As our society becomes wealthier, though, despite some economic hardships we may face, we've now reached a point where many of us can reevaluate what is important to us. We've discovered that people are increasingly willing to spend more to get higher quality food. Food from more responsible, more sustainable, and more ethical farms.

This is about what your values are—what you care about. Yes,

"Corporate livestock factory owners and management tout themselves as 'saviors' to the rural communities they target. Everyone is promised salvation: job creation for local inhabitants, increased tax revenues for local coffers, expanded markets for family farmers, and increased purchasing power for hometown businesses, with high-tech production for consumers. . . . However, the facts of the industry paint a different picture. Corporate livestock factories actually disable community development with self-serving contracts and tax breaks, market-monopolizing strategy, and few local purchases. . . . While communities naturally want to attract jobs, wealth, and capital for investment, transferring . . . [farm animal] production from local families to corporations facilitates and accelerates the extraction of wealth and capital from rural areas."[9]

affording a higher degree of welfare to animals raised for meat, eggs, and milk may cost more. If it were legal to employ child laborers in sweatshops, we could also drastically lower the cost and prices of most things that we manufacture and sell in the United States. But would that be acceptable? The obvious answer is no, it wouldn't. The only reason our abuse of animals is still tolerated is because most people aren't aware of it. If they were, they would be just as horrified as they were when they first became aware of what was happening with the exploitation of children in sweatshops.

Most people don't *want* to know because of the conflict and guilt they feel. But each one of us has a responsibility to be informed. Each one of us needs to be willing to look at the factory farms and their customary transport and slaughter practices, because we're choosing either to support them financially or to demand change with every purchasing decision we make.

That said, it can be somewhat hard for me to make the argument that we should pay more for our food when there is so much suffering and starvation occurring on this planet. But I oftentimes find that many of us, in a country where we spend a mere 8 percent of our income on food, are just using that as a rationalization to avoid dealing with the deeper ethical questions of animal welfare. Very simply, there are certain things that are just plain wrong. If a higher degree of animal welfare costs more, so be it. We should be willing to pay this price and shouldn't tolerate cruel and unethical treatment of farmed animals.

And, in fact, we aren't even paying the true cost—the actual financial cost—for meat, eggs, and milk. In the United States, economic conditions encourage the gross treatment of farmed animals as commodities in the form of government subsidies provided to agriculture.

Each year, the federal government doles out billions of dollars to the U.S. factory farming industries, especially to keep artificially low the prices of corn and soybeans, largely used as farmed animal feed. These large corporations receive taxpayer money, and while this does filter down to a certain extent to cheaper animal-based foods, it also distorts markets tremendously. These subsidies allow animal products to be sold far below their true costs.

Take corn subsidies, for example. Simply put, government subsidizing of corn subsidizes the factory farm animal production system, which is largely dependent on corn for feed. Eliminating corn subsides is a first step to valuing animals more accurately.

taxpayers are unknowingly subsidizing factory farms that benefit from artificially low prices for grains used as feed for industrially raised farmed animals. basically, when the price of grain is lower than its production cost, much of that difference is paid to grain farmers in the form of government subsidies that taxpayers cover. factory farms then buy grain at the unnaturally low market price, **making their irresponsible and welfare-unfriendly practices even more profitable.** below are the payouts, averaged from subsidies paid from 1997 to 2005.

sector	avg annual subsidy	avg annual subsidy per factory farm	avg annual subsidy per large factory farm	avg reduction in cost of production
chickens (raised for meat)	$1,250,000,000	$766,000	n/a	13%
dairy	$733,000,000	$233,000	$588,000	6%
eggs	$432,000,000	$388,000	n/a	13%
beef (feedlotted)	$500,000,000	$72,000	$2,200,000	5%
pigs	$945,000,000	$325,000	$5,010,000	15%
total	**$3,860,000,000**			

If those subsidies were taken away, animal products in general would become more expensive, and it is likely that less meat, eggs, and milk would be bought as a result—a positive outcome for our health, economy, environment, and the animals themselves. In addition, if corn were not subsidized by the government, higher welfare products like grass-fed beef would become more economically competitive in the market with beef from cattle confined on feedlots—another way of giving consumers a fair alternative.

This all would be good for farmed animals. Grazing animals, such as cows and steers, have not naturally evolved to eat high-energy foods like corn. Though it may force them to reach slaughter

Reports *The American Prospect*, "Halfway out the flat and arid Oklahoma panhandle, Texas County used to raise wheat, hay, cattle, and some—not many—hogs. In 1995, Seaboard Farms moved in to set up a giant pork slaughterhouse with more than $60 million in direct subsidies and tax breaks. To supply the plant, Seaboard set up hundreds of giant metal barns, each containing nearly 1,000 hogs. Texas County now raises more than a million hogs annually. Seaboard produces as much sewage as the city of Philadelphia, and it sits in open-air lagoons, some as large as 14 acres and as deep as 25 feet. Neighbors complain of intolerable stench, and everybody worries about water pollution."[10]

---

weight faster, which is a benefit for agribusiness, such unnatural diets have well-documented negative effects on the animals' digestive system and their overall health.

Eliminating subsidies that benefit industrial animal agribusiness would even benefit developing countries that currently struggle to compete with our cheap, subsidized food, which is being dumped into their markets and is destroying local indigenous agriculture industries that simply cannot compete on price. These are just some of the many immediate positive ripple effects that would occur from ending our agricultural subsidies. Yes, some animal-based food prices will rise, but the goal of our agricultural system should be more than simply producing cheap food below their true market costs, but also producing food ethically and sustainably.

The government should get out of subsidizing agriculture, period. But, of course, the cost of meat, eggs, and milk is more than exclusively financial, as you're reading in each chapter of this book. By focusing solely on making food as cheap as possible, we have often overlooked the grave environmental costs—which will some day be hard economic costs—for the low price of animal products, the cost of our declining rural communities, our health, and much more.

We need to create an alternative to the current system, which degrades our environment, our health, the lives of animals and people, and economies around the world. Because of the agricultural subsidies and the prevailing mindset that our food must cost as little as possible—consequences be damned—in the United States, we have both an unethical and unsustainable approach to producing meat, eggs, and milk. This single approach monopolizes the way we do things and for many people there is no reasonable alternative. Instead, they remain in denial about what's happening with animals. They resist raising their consciousness, resist finding out more.

But, we're living in a much more transparent world. It's going to be much more difficult to hide the facts and keep people ignorant about what's really going on, so I am actually very optimistic. I really think we're going to see major changes in the next decade.

One of the things I've learned growing Whole Foods Market is that you have to think bigger and think better. Continuing to act like factory-farmed meat, eggs, and milk cost only what they're marked on the shelf is good for none of us. We have to think creatively about our food and incorporate animal welfare and responsible farming practices into the calculations when we look at the real costs. The good news is that in the process, we will save much more than money alone.

underwriting factory farms

we can't say it any better or more powerfully than the union of concerned scientists did in its 2008 report, "cafos uncovered":

"the costs we pay as a society to support [factory farms]—in the form of taxpayer subsidies, pollution, harm to rural communities, and poorer public health—is much too high. . .the bottom line is that society is currently propping up an undesirable form of animal agriculture with enormous subsidies and lack of accountability for its externalized costs."

below are just a few of the many costs exacted by animal factories on the taxpayer bill:

the activity	the cost
distributing and applying manure to fields	$1,160,000,000 per year
falling property values	$26,000,000,000 (total loss)
animal agriculture's antibiotic overuse and its public health impacts	$1,500,000,000 – $3,000,000,000 per year
remediating manure "lagoon" leaks from pig and cow (dairy) facilities	$4,100,000,000 (total cost)

"The vast majority of meat, milk, and eggs in America comes from factory farms, which hardly resemble [the] bucolic family farms many Americans envision their food comes from. Instead, they are part of 'agribusiness,' where animals are mass produced for the slaughter house. And in the agribusiness, financial profitability takes priority over treating animals humanely."

—U.S. Congressman Jim Moran (VA)

4

Animals

Wayne Pacelle

Not long ago I visited my family in Connecticut and renewed some acquaintances who live near my Aunt Harriet's beautiful, semi-wooded property outside of New Haven. Growing up, I always enjoyed watching her wild neighbors—deer, raccoons, skunks, ducks, and geese. I kept an eye out for wild turkeys, too, groups of toms, hens, and poults foraging in the edge habitat so characteristic of suburban landscapes. When I was a kid, there were few wild turkeys in the East—hunters had seen to that—so I was always excited when I spotted one.

When I got into full-time animal protection work, I began visiting factory farms to see for myself how these animals are raised. Twenty years later, I am still amazed at the differences between the designs of nature and the designs of agribusiness. When I saw up to 10,000 domesticated turkeys raised in a single, filthy shed the length of a football field, they were a shadow of their natural selves.

Wild turkeys can run twenty-five miles an hour and in short bursts fly faster than fifty miles an hour. They live in flocks and forage more than twelve hours a day before retiring at night to roost in trees. They are so alert and fast that hunters dress in camouflage

Wayne Pacelle is the president and chief executive officer of the Humane Society of the United States, founder of Humane USA, and founder of the Humane Society Legislative Fund.

and face paint and use a device that mimics mating calls to lure the birds within shooting range. Despite their technological and strategic advantages, hunters often return home empty-handed because of the awareness and elusiveness of the birds.

Contrast them with the genetically manipulated turkeys used in agribusiness. With their massive breasts of fat and muscle, they are a caricature of the wild turkey. They are so bulky that toms cannot copulate without harming the hens, so breeding facilities "milk" the males for their semen and artificially inseminate the females.

Their legs, so well adapted for agility and speed in the wild, can barely hold up their enormous bodies. Walking and even standing can be painful. They suffer joint and hip problems, and their tendons and ligaments can even rupture. Even if they were not confined in buildings at a "stocking density" of 2.5 to 4 square feet per bird (compared to the 500 acres they may call home in the wild), flight is impossible for these grossly obese and heavily muscled birds. They live sedentary lives in an overcrowded shed, crammed wing-to-wing atop ammonia-laden excrement.

It's not only their physical form that's so exaggerated compared with wild turkeys. Their growth rate is insanely accelerated. Factory-farmed turkeys now weigh three times more than their wild brethren by just four months of age. A more compact "grow-out" period means producers can raise and process more turkey flocks within a year—which means more profits.

The welfare of farmed turkeys is so compromised that mortality rates of 7 to 10 percent are expected. Summing up agribusiness's priorities, an industry scientist said the "use of highly selected fast-growing strains is recommended because savings in feed costs and time far outweigh the loss of a few birds." The "few" birds he's referring to were actually 18 to 26 million turkeys dying on the factory farm in 2007 alone.

no. of large* animal production operations: 2002 and 1982

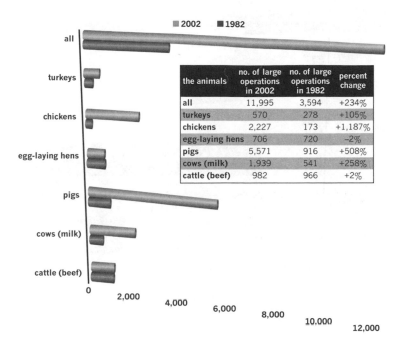

■ 2002   ■ 1982

the animals	no. of large operations in 2002	no. of large operations in 1982	percent change
all	11,995	3,594	+234%
turkeys	570	278	+105%
chickens	2,227	173	+1,187%
egg-laying hens	706	720	−2%
pigs	5,571	916	+508%
cows (milk)	1,939	541	+258%
cattle (beef)	982	966	+2%

It's not much different for chickens raised for meat. They are confined in the same type of massive, filthy sheds and are selectively bred for enlarged breasts and fast growth. These birds are slaughtered at just six weeks of age—down from eighty-four days fifty years ago. Just think of it. They now reach "market weight" in forty-two days and even earlier. According to researchers at the University of Arkansas's Division of Agriculture, "If you grew as fast as a chicken, you'd weigh 349 pounds at age 2."

This rapid growth places more stress on their already challenged bodies, producing not only tendon and joint ailments and crippling leg deformities, but also respiratory, circulatory, and pulmonary

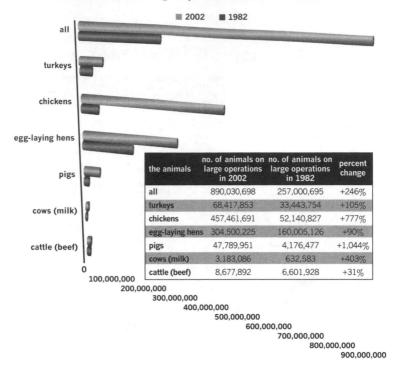

no. of animals raised on large* operations: 2002 and 1982

■ 2002 ■ 1982

the animals	no. of animals on large operations in 2002	no. of animals on large operations in 1982	percent change
all	890,030,698	257,000,695	+246%
turkeys	68,417,853	33,443,754	+105%
chickens	457,461,691	52,140,827	+777%
egg-laying hens	304,500,225	160,005,126	+90%
pigs	47,789,951	4,176,477	+1,044%
cows (milk)	3,183,086	632,583	+403%
cattle (beef)	8,677,892	6,601,928	+31%

disorders in birds who are the age equivalent of juveniles. Diseases often associated with old age are widespread in animals just a few weeks into their lives. Poultry scientist Dr. Ian Duncan notes that "[w]ithout a doubt, the biggest welfare problems for meat birds are those associated with rapid growth."

The numbers are staggering. Aided in part by today's ever-faster rates of growth, U.S. producers now raise more than 9 billion chickens a year, killing 1 million individual birds each hour to sate the average American's 80-birds-per-year consumption habit.

Jared Diamond notes in *Guns, Germs and Steel* that, in the

> "One of the best things modern animal agriculture has going for it is that most people . . . haven't a clue how animals are raised and processed. . . . In my opinion, if most urban meat eaters were to visit an industrial broiler house, to see how the birds are raised, and could see the birds being 'harvested' and then being 'processed' in a poultry processing plant, they would not be impressed and some, perhaps many of them, would swear off eating chicken and perhaps all meat."
>
> —Peter Cheeke, Ph.D., Oregon State University
> professor of animal agriculture, in his textbook
> *Contemporary Issues in Animal Agriculture*

10,000 years since humans first went down the path of domestication, we have successfully domesticated only some seventeen animal species—out of the thousands we've tried to conquer. And, in our own day, domestication has been carried to an extreme, morphing these animals to suit our economic designs. The industry has transformed animals into meat-, milk-, and egg-producing machines and overproductive "breeders." All standards of compassion and ethics have given way to productivity and efficiency.

Fifty years ago, animals were raised on small, diverse, family-run farms, and agricultural students learned "animal husbandry." Gradually, independent farmers lost out to intensive corporate factories, and animal husbandry gave way to "animal science," a change in terminology that signaled the new industrial ethos in the way we view and treat animals. Animals became "production units," and agribusiness's goal shifted to "growing" billions of

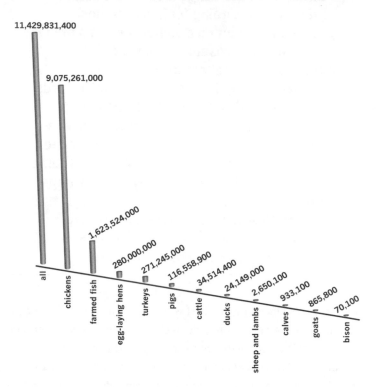

no. of animals killed per year in the u.s. industries: 11,429,831,400

- 11,429,831,400 — all
- 9,075,261,000 — chickens
- 1,623,524,000 — farmed fish
- 280,000,000 — egg-laying hens
- 271,245,000 — turkeys
- 116,558,900 — pigs
- 34,514,400 — cattle
- 24,149,000 — ducks
- 2,650,100 — sheep and lambs
- 933,100 — calves
- 865,800 — goats
- 70,100 — bison

animals as cheaply and quickly as possible in the smallest amount of space—all at the expense of the welfare of these individuals, who can suffer and experience joy just as much as the companion animals with whom we share our homes.

How did these changes—on the rural landscape, on academic campuses, and within farming industries as a whole—come about? Some of the causes can be seen in basic economic trends in animal agriculture. There has been enormous consolidation within the various industry sectors. Just look at the pig and turkey industries. In 1970, more than 700,000 farmers raised pigs. By 2006,

no. of animals killed per month in the u.s. industries: 952,485,950

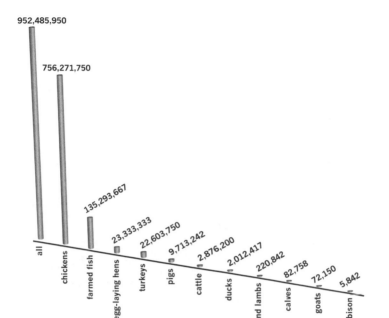

that number had been reduced by 90 percent, while the number of pigs raised skyrocketed. Similarly, in 1910, 870,000 farmers raised 3.7 million turkeys. In 2007, more than half of the nearly 265 million turkeys slaughtered in the United States were raised under contract in industrialized production facilities for only three companies.

It's been the same story in the chicken, egg, and dairy sectors. Only the cattle business has avoided this massive drop in producer numbers; there are still about one million operations that typically follow the formula of grazing cattle while they're young and then fattening them on massive amounts of corn, rather than grass, in

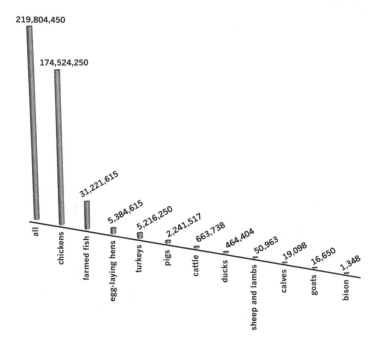

barren feedlots before they are slaughtered. Farming has changed to the point that the animals, the practices, and the ethos are virtually unrecognizable.

In addition to selective breeding for productivity traits and the mass, forced relocation of animals, except for cattle, from the outdoors to large, often windowless and typically barren, warehouse-like buildings, one of factory farming's greatest assaults is its intensive confinement methods that are particularly extreme in several sectors.

About 95 percent of the country's nearly 300 million egg-laying hens are crammed into small wire battery cages. Each cage con-

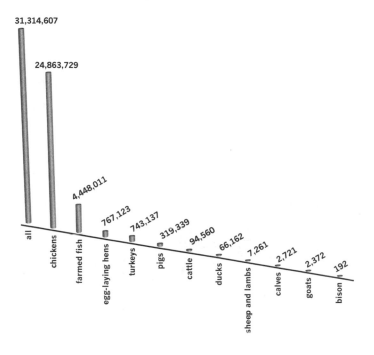

fines five to ten birds, and each hen is given about sixty-seven square inches of space—about two thirds the size of an 8½-by-11-inch piece of paper. They basically live all but on top of one another for about a year, unable to forage, dust-bathe, nest, or engage in any of the instinctive behaviors of free-roaming chickens. Inside battery cages, the hens can't even flap their wings.

Like other animals genetically manipulated for commercial imperatives, egg-laying hens now produce a mind-numbing yield. A factory-farmed hen produces about 250 eggs per year, though some lay 300 or more. That compares to about 100 eggs per hen a century ago. Their systems depleted by calcium loss and taxed by

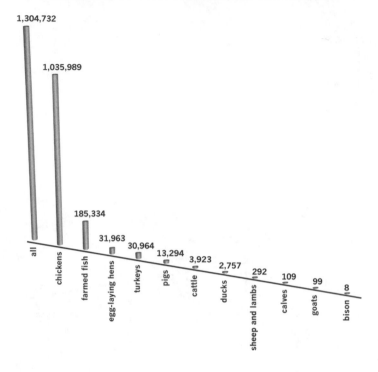

no. of animals killed per hour in the u.s. industries: 1,304,732

near-daily egg-laying, and their bones weakened further by virtual immobilization in restrictive battery cages, nearly 90 percent of these laying hens suffer from osteoporosis. This makes the birds highly susceptible to bone fractures, which can be deadly. One study, in fact, found that fractures were the main cause of mortality in caged hens.

The pig industry, as well, has radically departed from traditional farming methods. Most breeding sows are confined in individual gestation crates—two-by-seven-foot cages—that prevent them from even turning around. These curious, social animals—who, in an extensive system, would root around with their noses, forage,

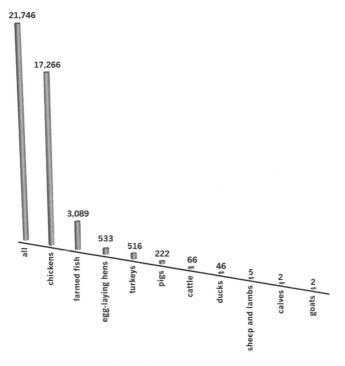

21,746

17,266

3,089

533

516

222

66

46

5

2

2

all

chickens

farmed fish

egg-laying hens

turkeys

pigs

cattle

ducks

sheep and lambs

calves

goats

build nests, and wallow in the mud—cannot engage in hardly any of their normal, instinctive behaviors. For nearly their entire four-month pregnancy, they can do nothing but stand and lie on concrete slatted floors, breathing in toxic ammonia emanating from massive waste pits. There is no positive stimulation and no social interaction. In such extreme confinement, their muscles atrophy, they lose bone mass, and they are often afflicted with lesions that are indicators of their terrible health and this unsanitary environment, not to mention the psychological torment they experience from such extreme restriction.

Before giving birth, the sow is moved to a farrowing crate—an

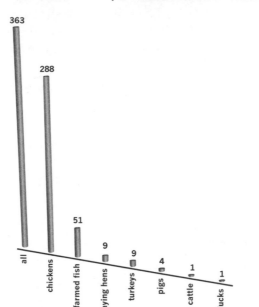

enclosure that separates her from her piglets but leaves her as severely restricted as she was in the gestation crate. There, the sow nurses her babies for a fraction of the time she would naturally, until they are prematurely weaned and begin to get fattened for slaughter. The sow, meanwhile, is reimpregnated and returned to the gestation crate for another four-month period.

Although pigs can live to be fifteen years old, breeding sows are typically "culled"—killed because they're no longer considered productive enough—after an average of 3.5 litters. Before it all ends for her, she may endure three or four successive pregnancies and farrowings—spending nearly two years crated so restrictively she cannot even turn around.

"[I]f the public knew more about the way in which agricultural and animal production infringes on animal welfare, the outcry would be louder. . . . [It is] more economically efficient to put a greater number of birds into each cage, accepting lower productivity per bird but greater productivity per cage. . . . [I]ndividual animals may 'produce,' for example gain weight, in part because they are immobile, yet suffer because of the inability to move. . . . Chickens are cheap, cages are expensive."[11]

> —Bernard E. Rollin, Ph.D., University Distinguished Professor, professor of philosophy, professor of animal sciences, professor of biomedical sciences, and University Bioethicist at the University of Colorado, and Commissioner of the Pew Commission on Industrial Farm Animal Production

These and other confinement systems have been shown time and again—through scientific inquiry, investigative exposé, and consumer polling—to be unacceptable, and citizens in Europe, North America, and beyond are organizing to get them out of the industry's playbook. The European Union has already voted to phase out conventional battery cages, gestation crates, and veal crates—the tiny stalls used to confine young male calves for veal. As of this writing, in the United States, legislation to ban gestation crates has been signed into law in Arizona, California, Maine, Michigan, Colorado, Florida, and Oregon.

In response, Smithfield Foods, the largest pig producer in the United States and in fact the world, has pledged to phase out

> "Some egg producers got rid of old hens by suffocating them in plastic bags or dumpsters. The more I learned about the egg industry the more disgusted I got. Some of the practices that had become 'normal' for this industry were overt cruelty. Bad had become normal. Egg producers had become desensitized to suffering. There is a point where economics alone must not be the sole justification for an animal production practice. When the egg producers asked me if I wanted cheap eggs, I replied, 'Would you want to buy a shirt if it was $5 cheaper and made by child slaves?' Hens are not human, but research clearly shows that they feel pain and can suffer."[12]
>
> —Temple Grandin, Ph.D., professor of animal science at Colorado State University, bestselling author, and livestock industry consultant

gestation crates over the next decade. Canada's largest pig producer, Maple Leaf Foods, made a similar pledge, and the industry seems to have now recognized that the public will not tolerate this extreme confinement system. Similarly, the American Veal Association, the trade group for its industry, announced that its producers would eliminate individual stalls for calves within a decade, and two of the largest U.S. veal producers, Strauss Veal and Marcho Farms, have already pledged to phase out crates due to animal welfare concerns.

Celebrity chef Wolfgang Puck recently implemented an historic animal welfare program in his multimillion-dollar company that

(agri) business as usual

univ. of arkansas: **"if you grew as fast as a chicken, you'd weigh 349 pounds at age 2."** muscle outpaces bone development, leading to skeletal weakness and leg deformities. **at any given moment, 2.5 million u.s. chickens have difficulty walking and experience pain.**

sows used for breeding are customarily confined in crates during their near-constant cycles of pregnancies and nursing— **unable even to turn around.** their piglets are **mutilated without any pain relief**—castrated, teeth clipped, ear notched, and tail docked.

cows are cyclically overtaxed to maximize industry milk yields. dr. john webster of the univ. of bristol school of veterinary science: **"the amount of work done by the cow in peak lactation is immense. to achieve a comparable high work rate a human would have to jog for about 6 hours a day, every day."**

at the hatchery, turkey chicks are typically mutilated without any pain relief—procedures including **de-snooding (slicing off the fleshy protuberance over the bird's beak), de-toeing, and de-beaking**—before they, like chickens raised for meat, are **overcrowded in barren sheds.**

in the u.s. catfish farming industry—the largest sector of domestic aquaculture, comprising approximately 83.4% of all fish farmed in the country and raising **more than 1.1 billion animals annually—mortality due to infectious disease can approach 30% of the population.**

an egg-laying hen needs an average of 120 in^2 of space to turn around, 137 in^2 to stretch her wings, 177 in^2 to ruffle her feathers, and 220 in^2 to flap her wings. on factory farms, **she is given an average of 67 in^2 of space for the entirety of her "productive" life.**

includes bans on eggs from caged laying hens, pork from producers who use gestation crates, and veal from producers who use veal crates. Fast-food giants Burger King and Wendy's, among others, recently announced a number of corporate policies to improve farmed animal welfare, including purchasing some of its eggs from producers who do not confine hens in cages as well as some pork from producers who do not confine sows in gestation crates, and giving purchasing preference for chicken meat from plants

> "Is it more profitable to grow the biggest bird and have increased mortality due to heart attacks, ascites, and leg problems, or should birds be grown slower so that birds are smaller, but have fewer heart, lung and skeletal problems? . . . [S]imple calculations suggest that it is better to get the weight and ignore the mortality." [13]

> "Forget the pig is an animal. Treat him just like a machine in a factory." [14]

> "The breeding sow should be thought of, and treated as, a valuable piece of machinery whose function is to pump out baby pigs like a sausage machine." [15]

> "Male dairy calves are used in the veal industry. Dairy cows must give birth to continue producing milk, but male dairy calves are of little or no value to the dairy farmer. A small percentage are raised to maturity and used for breeding." [16]

---

that use controlled atmosphere killing, a method found to be far less inhumane than the customary electric stunning slaughter of birds.

Moving industry away from systems that clearly abuse animals has been challenging, but the tide is turning. Our work, however, doesn't end with on-farm victories. Compared to the "production" period—which constitutes the vast majority of an animal's life—transport and slaughter are brief. But these final phases are fraught with stress and often cause untold suffering.

The more than 9 billion chickens and 270 million turkeys killed for meat each year in the United States must be caught and crated before they're stacked onto massive slaughter-bound trucks. "Catchers" manually gather the birds by physically grabbing them, carrying several at a time by their legs and even wings, and throwing them into crates. During an average shift, a single chicken catcher lifts and crates as many as 1,500 birds in an hour. With workers moving at such a frenzied pace, the animals can—and do—sustain severe injuries, including broken legs and wings, internal hemorrhaging, ruptured tendons, and dislocated hips. A number of studies report that as many as 20 to 30 percent suffer injury during the collection process.

Crated and on the truck, the birds are denied food, water, and even protection from the elements. Wholly unfamiliar with the outdoors—wind, sunlight, rain, and myriad noises—the birds experience shock and fear. Transport can even result in death. Birds may die en route from infectious disease, heart and circulatory disorders, and trauma experienced during catching and crating. In fact, dead-on-arrival (DOA) estimates for chickens range from 0.19 to 0.46 percent, which means a staggering 17 to 41 million birds die during transport every year.

Pigs, cattle, and other farmed animals experience similar conditions during transport—overcrowded confinement and lack of basic provisions for their health and well-being. Trucking live animals with already weakened immune systems, not to mention cardiovascular, skeletal, and respiratory disorders, is not only an animal protection issue, but a public health concern, as these animals are much more susceptible to disease, existing infections, and new pathogens.

At the slaughter plant, animals face a range of assaults,

including aggressive handling, inefficient stunning, and even regaining consciousness during slaughter. In a devastating exposé in the *Washington Post* in 2001, Pulitzer Prize–winning journalist Joby Warrick reported that the U.S. Department of Agriculture was not shutting down noncompliant slaughterers, cattle were being skinned alive, and plant managers instilled atmospheres in which processing speed trumped the welfare of animals.

Even more shocking is the fact that birds, who make up more than 95 percent of all land-based animals killed for food, are not afforded the protections under the federal Humane Methods of Slaughter Act, as interpreted by the USDA. As a result, the billions of birds killed annually are not even rendered insensible to pain before they are shackled, electrically stunned, and their throats are slit.

Nonambulatory cattle, also known as "downers," are routinely subjected to horrendous mistreatment. Primarily so-called "spent" dairy cows, these animals, exhausted and broken, are unable even to walk and stand on their own. On January 30, 2008, my organization, the Humane Society of the United States, released the findings of an undercover investigation at a cattle slaughter plant in California that documented downed cows being rammed with the blades of a forklift, dragged with chains pulled by heavy machinery, suffering simulated drowning as water from a high-pressure hose was forced down their throats and nostrils, and repeatedly electrically shocked and beaten—all in attempts to get them on their feet to walk to slaughter. The footage of blatant animal cruelty alarmed the nation and, indeed, the world. Within one month, two employees of the slaughter plant were charged with animal cruelty; the nation's largest-ever recall was issued; a $100-million-dollar company was shut down; Congressional hearings were held; and lawmakers and consumers alike questioned how these events could have occurred.

As of this writing, the USDA has committed to closing—finally—a loophole in the law that allowed the torment of these animals who couldn't even stand or walk. We're hopeful that we will see an end to the slaughter of downed cattle, a long-fought battle, yet that promised ban still will not apply to pigs or other farmed animals. It is, however, a significant step in the right direction.

There are more animals used in food production than all other animal-use industries put together, yet the laws to protect animals raised for food are weak or nonexistent and often not enforced. While we've achieved some improvements, agribusiness concerns and their allies in state and federal government are powerful forces that resist change. Some of the fastest change is occurring in the retail sector, as food service providers and consumers are demanding an end to some of the worst cruelties factory farmers have instituted as customary agricultural practice. And of course, every person has the power in his or her life to make change by making food choices with the animals in mind.

For my part, the many cruelties I have witnessed in twenty-plus years of animal advocacy have only reaffirmed my convictions about the importance of kindness to animals and the great possibilities of legal reform and personal transformation. Human beings can do such great harm to the animal world, but we are also capable of doing such great good. Animals have a way of bringing out both the worst and the best in the human heart—our most selfish and callous instincts, and our most generous and noble. I've witnessed a lot more of the latter in my work than the former. And I believe more than ever that showing respect and compassion for animals is one of the finest marks we can leave in this world.

> "Once our personal connection to what is wrong becomes clear, then we have to choose: we can go on as before, recognizing our dishonesty and living with it the best we can, or we can begin the effort to change the way we think and live."
>
> —Wendell Berry, Kentucky farmer and writer

5

Climate Change

Danielle Nierenberg and Meredith Niles

Climate change is undoubtedly the most pressing environmental issue of our time. Glaciers are melting, arctic tundra is thawing, hurricanes and other extreme weather events are occurring more frequently, and penguins, polar bears, and countless other plant and animal species are struggling to survive in the face of rising temperatures. Thanks primarily to the efforts of the Nobel Peace Prize–winning Intergovernmental Panel on Climate Change (IPCC), whose scientists were among the first to document the growth in global greenhouse gas emissions (GHGs), and the perseverance of environmentalists, people worldwide are more aware than ever of how human actions contribute to climate change. Increasingly, we understand that we drive too much and bike too little, leave our lights and computers on when we're not using them, and buy clothes, electronic gadgets, and other products that we may not *really* need—all of which contribute to rising GHG emissions and increasing environmental and health problems.

While embracing a "greener" lifestyle can play a significant role in reducing GHG emissions and decreasing our dependence on fossil fuels, mitigation strategies cannot rest with shifts in our modes

Danielle Nierenberg, M.S., is a senior researcher at the Worldwatch Institute and a co-project director of *State of World 2011: Nourishing the Planet*. Meredith Niles is the coordinator of the Cool Foods Campaign, a national initiative of the CornerStone Campaign and the Center for Food Safety.

> **Dr. Rajendra Pachauri, chair of the Intergovernmental Panel on Climate Change and Nobel Prize winner, on reducing meat consumption to fight climate change:** "In terms of immediacy of action and the feasibility of bringing about reductions in a short period of time, it clearly is the most attractive opportunity. . . . Give up meat for one day [a week] initially, and decrease it from there."[17]

of transportation, remembering to turn off electricity-draining lights and machinery, or curbing our consumer purchases. Indeed, the most significant contributor to greenhouse gas emissions is one we "tap"—at every meal.

Of all greenhouse gas emissions globally, the Food and Agriculture Organization of the United Nations (FAO) has determined that the entire transportation sector is second to the farmed animal sector. That is, the meat, egg, and dairy industries are responsible for even more devastating GHG emissions than the world's cars, airplanes, motorbikes, and all other transport. To meaningfully reduce our impact on the environment, we must change the way we eat and we must change the way we farm.

Increasingly, the more than 60 billion land-based animals raised and killed for human consumption are reared in intensive, industrialized production facilities, and every aspect of factory farming—from the fertilizers and pesticides used to grow animal feed and the energy required to operate automated production facilities to the clearing of rainforests in the Amazon for soy production and pasture land—emits GHGs into the atmosphere. These and other "ingredients" of today's meat, egg, and dairy production are heav-

Which one of these contributes more to

Global Warming?

It's not the one that starts a car.

Celebrating Animals | Confronting Cruelty

THE HUMANE SOCIETY
OF THE UNITED STATES

humanesociety.org/food

ily dependent on fossil fuels. Animals raised in industrialized operations, for example, are fed a diet consisting mainly of corn and soybeans that require massive amounts of pesticides, herbicides, and, particularly, artificial fertilizers. Indeed, fertilizer production for feed crops alone contributes some 41 million tons of carbon dioxide (CO_2) annually—the equivalent of that produced by nearly 7 million cars.

The European Parliament recognizes that "the cultivation of cereals and soya feed for livestock is responsible for substantial greenhouse gas emissions" and "considers that a switch from intensive livestock production to extensive sustainable systems should be encouraged while total meat consumption needs to be reduced, in particular in industrialised countries." [18]

Heating and cooling the massive confinement operations that dot the U.S. landscape—and increasingly parts of Asia, Latin America, and the Caribbean—also results in several million tons of CO_2 emissions. In the past, factory farms were typically located close to where feed was grown, but low transportation costs have allowed confinement facilities to be located far from fields of corn and soybeans. In some regions, including China, factory farms are cropping up next to cities, requiring long-distance transportation of feed.

We've known for decades that farmed animal production has also had disastrous impacts on fragile forest ecosystems and the biodiversity they contain, including an untold number of plant and animals species that have not yet been identified. In the 1980s, environmentalists in industrialized countries blamed McDonald's and other fast-food chains for buying beef produced from animals raised on previously forested areas in Latin America. Contrary to popular belief, however, most of the beef from slaughtered cattle who had been raised in the rainforest was not for middle-class Americans, but for domestic consumption in the countries where the animals lived. Unfortunately, today, this is changing, as areas of the Amazon and other parts of South and Central America are be-

roasting the atmosphere, one chicken at a time

beef gets a bad wrap when it comes to the environment—and rightfully so when you consider the industry's culpability in deforestation, pollution, and greenhouse gas emissions. but what about chicken? **you could drive to the moon and back 114,000 times and still have released less carbon than the u.s. chicken industry does annually.** if you want to reduce your ecological footprint, eating chickens instead of cattle is not the answer.

year	u.s. population	per-capita u.s. chicken consumption	CO_2 emissions to produce chickens consumed in the u.s. in miles driven by a 24-mpg car
1970	203,302,031	36.6 lbs	16,600,000,000 miles
1980	226,545,805	45.8 lbs	23,040,000,000 miles
1990	248,709,873	59.5 lbs	18,300,000,000 miles
2000	281,421,906	76.9 lbs	32,900,000,000 miles
2010	299,862,000	83.5 lbs	55,800,000,000 miles

ing cleared for export beef production and the production of soy for animal feed. David Kaimowitz, director general of the Center for International Forestry Research, reported in 2004 that rapid growth in Brazilian beef overseas has been accelerating destruction of the Amazon and that the area of forest loss increased from 41.5 million hectares in 1990 to 58.7 million hectares—an area twice the size of Portugal—in 2000. "In a nutshell," said Kaimowitz, "cattle ranchers are making mincemeat out of Brazil's Amazon rainforests."

Loss of biodiversity from these forests is only part of the problem, as clearing forests for pasture land and to grow feed crops releases some 2.4 billion tons of CO_2 into the atmosphere annually. Since South American forests and grasslands (which are also in danger from cattle ranching, the construction of slaughter plants, and soy production) act as "carbon sinks," they can soak up and sequester CO_2, which is crucial to lessening our emissions. When forests and grasslands are cut down, however, all of their stored carbon is

Reports *The Lancet*, the world's leading general medical journal, "For the world's higher-income populations, greenhouse-gas emissions from meat-eating warrant the same scrutiny as do those from driving and flying, especially in view of the great warming potential of methane in the short-to-medium term."[19]

---

released into the atmosphere. A Greenpeace report issued in 2008 indicated that land conversion like this is the number-one contributor of GHG emissions from agriculture throughout the world.

Yet, CO_2 is only one of the greenhouse gases created from industrial animal agriculture. Nitrous oxide and methane, with nearly 300 and 23 times the global warming potential of CO_2, respectively, are also emitted, mostly from the billions of tons of manure produced annually by farm animals worldwide. In the United States alone, cattle, pigs, chickens, turkeys, and other animals raised on factory farms generate approximately 454 million tonnes of solid and liquid waste.

Natural manure, when used to fertilize soil, is a key part of healthy, sustainable farms and landscapes. One of the biggest crimes of industrial animal agriculture may be its move from pasture-based farming to indoor confinement. As animals have been herded inside into massive "grow-out" sheds and warehouse-like facilities, it is impossible for their manure to be used as fertilizer. The huge quantities of excrement produced on factory farms exceed the amount of nearby land available to absorb it, transforming manure from a valuable agricultural resource into a toxic waste that threatens soil, water, air quality, and climate. Storing and disposing of these mountains of manure can lead

for planetary health, forget about counting calories & carbs. count CO$_2$e.

we used *bon appétit*'s carbon calculator (thanks!) to share with you the "points" of some typical meals. CO$_2$e (or carbon dioxide equivalent) is an internationally recognized measure of the amount of global warming from greenhouse gases like methane. 1 "point" equals 1 gram of CO$_2$e.

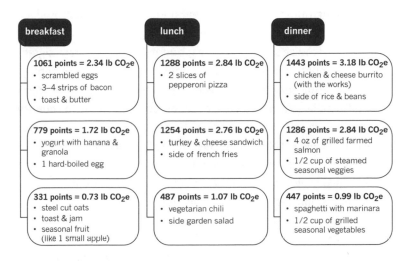

breakfast

1061 points = 2.34 lb CO$_2$e
- scrambled eggs
- 3–4 strips of bacon
- toast & butter

779 points = 1.72 lb CO$_2$e
- yogurt with banana & granola
- 1 hard-boiled egg

331 points = 0.73 lb CO$_2$e
- steel cut oats
- toast & jam
- seasonal fruit (like 1 small apple)

lunch

1288 points = 2.84 lb CO$_2$e
- 2 slices of pepperoni pizza

1254 points = 2.76 lb CO$_2$e
- turkey & cheese sandwich
- side of french fries

487 points = 1.07 lb CO$_2$e
- vegetarian chili
- side garden salad

dinner

1443 points = 3.18 lb CO$_2$e
- chicken & cheese burrito (with the works)
- side of rice & beans

1286 points = 2.84 lb CO$_2$e
- 4 oz of grilled farmed salmon
- 1/2 cup of steamed seasonal veggies

447 points = 0.99 lb CO$_2$e
- spaghetti with marinara
- 1/2 cup of grilled seasonal vegetables

to significant pollution of the air and water, and is producing excessive amounts of GHGs.

Animal agriculture, including billions of pigs, chickens, and cattle raised with industrial-style methods, contributes more than one-third of all annual methane emissions, with the rest coming from landfills, rice cultivation, and other natural sources. While individual cows don't emit that much methane—just about 80 to 110 kilograms each year—the more than 1 billion ruminant animals worldwide produce untenable amounts of methane during enteric fermentation, the digestive process that breaks down food in their multiple stomachs. In fact, ruminant animals produce 86 million metric tons of methane worldwide.

Enteric fermentation, however, doesn't have to be that gassy. Cattle confined in feedlots or on dairy factory farms are fed a very unnatural diet of grain and soybeans that can cause a range of illnesses among cattle and may also lead to more methane emissions. Eating a more natural, lower-energy diet composed of grasses and other forages—what cattle are meant to eat—can, according to the U.S. Environmental Protection Agency, produce manure with about half of the potential to generate methane.

Animals raised for meat, eggs, and milk also generate significant amounts of nitrous oxide through their manure. A 10 percent rise in nitrous oxide emissions in the United States between 1990 and 2005 has been traced, at least partly, to changes in the poultry industry, including an increase in the population of birds raised for meat and eggs. For example, just on the Delmarva Peninsula—the area where Delaware, Maryland, and Virginia meet—more than 500 million birds are raised each year, compromising the air quality of that region and affecting the climate.

Changing consumption patterns are also playing a big role in emissions as countries like China and India are fast becoming consumers of not only huge amounts of energy—China in 2008 became the biggest emitter of CO_2—but also of meat, eggs, and dairy. According to the International Food Policy Research Institute, per-capita meat and dairy consumption in China has more than doubled since 1983, and the nation is the largest producer and consumer of pork in the world; India, on the other hand, is the world's leading milk producer and is rapidly expanding its chicken and egg factory farms. Unfortunately, it appears that China and India are not looking to Western Europe as an example of how to build and practice more low-carbon, energy-efficient systems and lifestyles—they're looking to the United States, undoubtedly the most notorious polluter on the planet.

Despite continual challenges on the climate front, there is a growing and inspiring trend of businesses and consumers taking very concrete steps to curb climate change. In the United States, farmers are both creating and taking advantage of the growing market for more environmentally sustainable and animal welfare–friendly meat, egg, and dairy products. The number of farms raising pasture-raised cattle, for example, has grown from several dozen to more than 1,000 over the last decade. Countless other farmers are bringing free-range, organic eggs, pork, cheese, and other products to the thousands of farmers markets that have cropped up all over country in the last fifteen years. Indeed, organic farming practices may have the greatest potential to help reduce GHGs in the world of agriculture. The Organic Consumers Association encourages consumers to seek out locally produced, seasonal organic foods, as well as vegetarian fare, to combat climate change. Raising cattle slaughtered for beef organically on grass—and not on feedlots or factory farms—may emit 40 percent less CO_2, methane, and nitrous oxide and consume up to 85 percent less energy than conventional raising practices.

Consumers are also taking advantage of learning more about where their food comes from and the environmental impacts of its production by using carbon calculators, like the one recently designed by *Bon Appétit*. Its online calculator allows consumers to compare the impacts of different foods or meals, such as the difference between an omelet with cheese and meat compared to one made with eggs alone, or the carbon footprint of a spinach and tofu salad or a bean burrito compared to roast beef or chicken.

Shoppers can also visit Climate Counts, a website that ranks different companies on their commitment to combating climate change. Not surprisingly, most fast-food companies don't score very well, lacking concrete initiatives to control GHGs from their operations and/or the foods they choose to serve their customers.

McDonald's Corporation, along with agribusiness giant Cargill and the environmental group Greenpeace, however, are working to address how to stop GHGs resulting from deforestation. In a collaborative effort with McDonald's, Cargill—which had been supplying the fast-food chain with Brazilian soy for chicken feed in factory farms—and Greenpeace persuaded soy traders to enter a two-year moratorium on purchases of soy from newly deforested regions.

While rankings, carbon calculators, moratoria, and laws are useful tools, ultimately we all must address climate change and those impacting industries with our own individual choices. We have the power to decide what kind of agriculture and what kind of climate we want. When it comes to our food, reducing or eliminating animal products is one of the most effective ways individuals can fight climate change. A recent study by Carnegie Mellon University demonstrated that nearly 60 percent of all emissions in the food system were from animal products. "The answer is not," according to the Natural Resources Defense Council, "milk in place of meat, but a more plant-based diet overall." And it's not only environmentalists espousing the benefits of a less animal product–intensive diet. *Time* magazine concluded that, "given the amount of energy consumed raising, shipping and selling livestock, a 16-oz. [450 g] T-bone is like a Hummer on a plate."

Fighting climate change by eating fewer meat, egg, and dairy products can also have benefits for human health. An article published by *The Lancet* in September 2007 advocates a reduction in meat consumption to 90 grams (3.18 ounces) per person per day (roughly the equivalent of a single beef hamburger patty), both to reduce GHG emissions and to promote better human health.

Ten or fifteen years ago, people who installed compact fluorescent light bulbs or biked to work were considered radical environmentalists, but now those habits are widely touted for their environmental benefits. Now, day by day, growing numbers of us are recognizing that fighting climate change and reducing environmental problems begins with the way we eat. Reducing or eliminating meat, egg, and dairy consumption, or, at the very least, choosing not to support industrialized factory-farmed products and, instead, selecting organic products from pasture-based farming systems, is a crucial part of reducing our environmental footprint. Animal agribusiness cannot be business as usual, whether for the welfare of animals or the devastating effects of climate change. We must and can do better.

"Go with plants. Eating a plant-based diet is healthiest. Choose plenty of vegetables, fruits, whole grains, and healthy fats, like olive and canola oil." [20]

—Harvard School of Public Health Nutrition Source

6

Children's Health

Sara Kubersky and Tom O'Hagan

Our paths to a cruelty-free lifestyle were different: while Tom was guided by a philosophical and ethical objection to the violence inherent in the industries that raised and killed animals for meat, eggs, and milk, Sara was led by a direct, emotional response to the suffering of animals. After we individually and independently became vegan, we met while Tom was shopping for cruelty-free shoes at MooShoes, the Manhattan vegan boutique owned by Sara and her sister Erica. Sara helped Tom find nonleather shoes—both then and now.

Years later, after we married, we decided it was time for us to share our lives and our family of four-legged companions with a child. When our son Leo was born, there was never any debate between us that we would raise him in the healthiest and most compassionate way we knew. We knew we wanted to raise him just as we had chosen to live. Our decision was based on a simple question: what parents don't want the very best for their kids? Our answer was equally simple: raising children who are compassionate to animals—ethically, in action, and dietarily—gives them the healthiest possible start on life.

Some may disagree that animal-free diets are the most

Sara Kubersky is the co-owner of MooShoes, a cruelty-free shoe store in Manhattan. Tom O'Hagan formerly co-owned Chainsaw Safety Records and currently blogs about film, books, and music.

healthful, often without even looking into the overwhelming evidence that proves otherwise. While we are not physicians (though Sara studied nutrition before opening MooShoes), Dr. Benjamin Spock, the most famous pediatrician of all time, was. And what did the world's leading authority on child care have to say about feeding meat, eggs, and dairy to kids? Before he died at ninety-four, the good doctor embraced veganism. In his final edition of *Dr. Benjamin Spock's Baby and Child Care*, one of the bestselling books in history (second only to the Bible), Dr. Spock wrote that "children who grow up getting their nutrition from plant foods rather than meats have a tremendous health advantage. They are less likely to develop weight problems, diabetes, high blood pressure and some forms of cancer."

Dr. Spock also recommended against children—or adults for that matter—drinking milk, which he said "causes intestinal blood loss, allergies, indigestion and contributes to some cases of childhood diabetes." Before Leo was born, we knew we wouldn't feed him milk-based formulas for ethical reasons, and Dr. Spock's condemnation of dairy consumption confirmed for us that we were right in choosing to breastfeed our son. In fact, cow's milk is well-recognized as the leading cause of iron-deficiency anemia in infants and children in the United States. The inflammation milk can cause in the maturing gut of babies can cause tiny bleeds in the intestinal lining, leading to blood loss and anemia. Leo had trouble latching in his first weeks, but we kept trying because we knew that human breast milk is perfectly designed for baby humans, just as cow's milk is perfectly designed for baby calves.

Cow's milk is also the leading cause of pediatric digestive complaints and is the single leading cause of food allergies in children. We aren't only talking sniffles and tummy aches. Type 1 diabetes has been linked to dairy consumption during infancy. Just as we were never meant to drink a dog's milk or a donkey's milk, we, as a species, were never meant to drink the milk of cattle. Scientists think that when a baby's immune system mounts a response to this invasion of foreign cow proteins, the baby's own pancreas may be damaged in the assault, resulting in a diabetic insulin–dependence for life.

Kids are supposed to grow up healthy—not constantly suffering from recurrent ear infections, stomachaches, headaches, and runny noses. Animal products have been linked to childhood asthma, allergies, and infection. Most parents probably just don't know any better because, unfortunately, most pediatricians probably don't either.

Not only may kids who eat healthy vegan diets get sick less often, veg kids studied in the United States grow up taller and leaner than their peers, and studies in the United Kingdom even suggest that veg kids are smarter. Not only have studies shown that vegetarian kids tend to develop higher IQs, the reverse has also been shown to be true: Kids with higher IQs are more likely to choose to become vegetarian themselves. Smart kids indeed!

Starting children out right gives them an early lead on developing enduring, healthy eating habits. Studies of vegetarian teens show that they are much more likely to meet healthy eating goals of consuming less saturated fat, more fiber, and more fruits and vegetables, rather than consuming more soda and junk food.

A healthful and humane diet does more than just present a good role model as children grow older. Research on what's called "flavor programming" shows the remarkable effect that exposing babies to the tastes of different foods can have on their future likes and dislikes. Flavors of foods can get into breast milk and even amniotic fluid before birth. Eating healthy foods during pregnancy can set up children for a lifelong love of healthy foods.

People unfamiliar with cruelty-free diets immediately think such a diet is restrictive in its choices. But, as Leo started on solids, we

how do they match up in the "healthy people 2010" objectives set for the nation by the u.s. department of health and human services? findings from the largest comparison study of veg and non-veg adolescents.

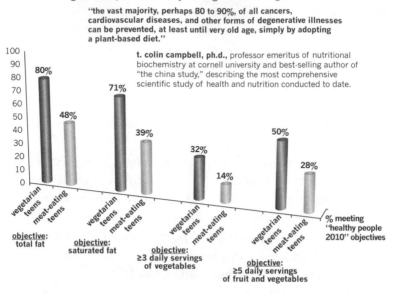

"the vast majority, perhaps 80 to 90%, of all cancers, cardiovascular diseases, and other forms of degenerative illnesses can be prevented, at least until very old age, simply by adopting a plant-based diet."

t. colin campbell, ph.d., professor emeritus of nutritional biochemistry at cornell university and best-selling author of "the china study," describing the most comprehensive scientific study of health and nutrition conducted to date.

objective: total fat

objective: saturated fat

objective: ≥3 daily servings of vegetables

objective: ≥5 daily servings of fruit and vegetables

% meeting "healthy people 2010" objectives

were amazed by how many different foods he enjoyed. Plus, not relying on animal products such as milk or cheese in his early eating experiences opened him up to wonderfully healthy and tasty food choices not typically associated with infant food, such as avocado, mango, asparagus, quinoa, and tofu. As Leo graduated from eating baby food to eating what's on our own plates, we became even more attuned to our own food choices. If Leo was eating what we were, we needed to make sure our meals were as healthy as possible.

We have the fattest generation of kids in history, yet the Standard American Diet—aptly known as SAD—is still embraced by families from coast to coast. Studies now show that more than half of the children and young adults in the United States already have

> **"Appropriately planned vegan, lacto-vegetarian, and lacto-ovo-vegetarian diets satisfy [the] nutrient needs of infants, children, and adolescents and promote normal growth. Vegetarian diets in childhood and adolescence can aid in the establishment of lifelong healthy eating patterns and can offer some important nutritional advantages. Vegetarian children and adolescents have lower intakes of cholesterol, saturated fat, and total fat and higher intakes of fruits, vegetables, and fiber than nonvegetarians. Vegetarian children have also been reported to be leaner and to have lower serum cholesterol levels."** [21]
>
> —American Dietetic Association, the world's largest association of food and nutrition professionals

the beginnings of heart disease in their arteries—a greater than one-in-two odds that our kids have started hurting their hearts. It should come as no surprise that adult cancers and heart attacks can be caused by childhood diets. The famous Bogalusa Heart Study found that high animal fat intake early in life is strongly predictive of later heart disease. Meanwhile, vegetarian children consistently have been shown to have healthier cholesterol levels. Eating vegan foods is all about heart, and raising animal-friendly children sets them up for life with a clear conscience—and clear arteries.

For girls, healthy and humane diets are critical for so many specific reasons. Breast tissue is especially sensitive to cancer triggers in the childhood and teenage years. In previous centuries, the average age of onset of puberty was seventeen—now, on average, girls start their periods at age twelve. This trend has been blamed in part on the dramatic increase of animal foods in the diet. Earlier puberty and breast development mean more lifetime estrogen exposure, which can mean higher risk of breast cancer later in life.

Cows raised organically may not be injected with bovine growth hormone, but they still produce milk filled with natural growth and sex hormones, such as estrogen, progesterone, and testosterone. Milk from a cow has been specially designed by nature to turn a 65-pound calf into a 500-pound cow or bull in just a single year. So maybe milk does a body good if you need to gain a few hundred extra pounds, but, otherwise, it might not be the best choice.

According to the USDA, about one in six U.S. cows has clinical mastitis, a painful udder infection that can drip pus and blood into the animal's milk. The United States has the highest permitted upper limit of milk pus cell concentration in the world—almost twice the international standard of allowable pus cells—a shocking (and incredibly unappetizing) 180 million per cup, compared to 96 million per cup in Europe. The dairy industry insists that this presents no health hazard, because any bacteria present would be killed by pasteurization. Even if the pus *is* cooked, though, do we want to feed it to our children?

It's like the meat industry with its irradiation. Instead of cleaning up its own act, it's more cost-effective just to irradiate the meat and kill off any bacteria and viruses present in the fecal material contaminating the carcass. But even if it's sterilized, why serve up fecal matter in *any* kitchen.

By choosing not to eat animals, their milk, or their eggs, especially in the age of modern hygiene and water supply purification, we are not being naturally exposed to enough B12, a vitamin produced by bacteria that inhabit many of the animals people eat, so we make sure to get it in fortified foods such as the soymilk we drink every day (which, incidentally, is fortified with vitamin D, too).

What about pesticides? Parents are so vigilant about keeping kids away from poisons and toxins, but what about the pesticides that can collect in one's body and have been linked with a number of different cancers? What people don't tend to realize is that pesticide residues can build up in the bodies of animals as well, and so we can get a lifetime of pesticide accumulation with every bite of a fish, a chicken, or other animals seen as food. Animal products can have more than ten times the pesticide levels of plant foods. This is another area where vegetarians shine. There was a report in the *New England Journal of Medicine* that found that the levels of pesticides in the breast milk of vegetarians were far lower than the national average. Looking at the levels of a number of pesticides and industrial pollutants, the researchers concluded that "vegetarian levels were only 1 to 2 percent as high as the average levels in the United States." Other studies have shown the same trend: Vegetarians have the lowest levels of toxic chemicals like pesticides and PCBs in their breast milk, whereas mothers eating fatty fish were found to have the highest.

This is separate from the concern over the levels of toxic heavy metals in aquatic animals. The Environmental Protection Agency (EPA) estimates that annually in the United States, up to 600,000 children are born at risk for lower intelligence and learning problems due to mercury exposure because their mothers ate fish. This led to the current EPA warning that cautions young children, pregnant and breastfeeding women, and even women just planning to get pregnant, to severely limit the consumption of many types of fish and fish products, like canned tuna, and to stay away from some other types of fish completely.

Unborn children and breastfeeding infants are especially susceptible to the toxic effects of pollutants. The most powerful known carcinogen in the world is probably a man-made industrial toxin called dioxin. When you hear something referred to as toxic waste on the news, they're probably talking about dioxins. Through food alone, nonvegan Americans are getting up to twenty times the maximum allowable daily dioxin exposure set by the EPA. Putting aside the dioxins present in cigarette smoke, the number-one source of dioxin exposure for Americans is via the diet, in chickens and eggs, fish, dairy, and other animal products. Nursing infants with nonvegan mothers can get more than sixty times the maximum tolerable dose of dioxins! Breast is still best, even when mothers expose their babies to these levels of toxins, but vegan breast milk is better.

In 2003, the most prestigious scientific body in the country, the National Academy of Sciences, released a damning report on the amount of dioxins in the U.S. food supply. Its number-one recommendation was for our kids to reduce their consumption of all fatty animal foods. This is because dioxins are stored in animal fat, and U.S. omnivores are getting more than twenty times the tolerable daily dose in their diet. Twenty. In the United States, millions of tons of fat are scraped from the carcasses of farmed animals and put straight back into animal feed. We've turned natural herbivores like cows into meat-eaters and have made them, along with pigs, chickens, and other animals, into cannibals as well. Fat trimmings from those animal carcasses get fed to other animals, and the dioxin levels get higher and higher.

In 1997, researchers at the University of New York Health Sciences Center published a study measuring the levels of industrial pollutants in fast food. They sent to the lab McDonald's Big Macs, slices of Pizza Hut cheese pizza, KFC's Original Recipe chicken, and scoops of Häagen Dazs ice cream thrown in for dessert. They found quite a toxic soup: PCBs, dioxins, and even pesticides like DDT, a pesticide considered so toxic it was banned decades ago.

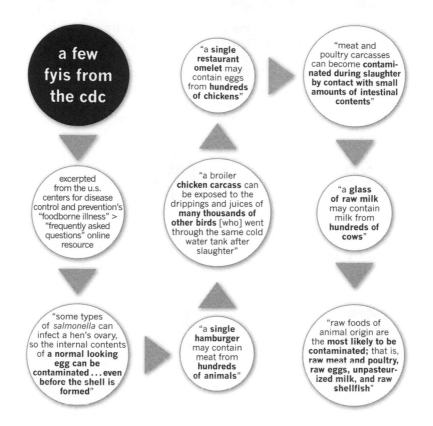

a few fyis from the cdc

"a **single restaurant omelet** may contain eggs from **hundreds of chickens**"

"meat and poultry carcasses can become **contaminated during slaughter** by contact with small amounts of intestinal contents"

excerpted from the u.s. centers for disease control and prevention's "foodborne illness" > "frequently asked questions" online resource

"a broiler **chicken carcass** can be exposed to the drippings and juices of **many thousands of other birds** [who] went through the same cold water tank after slaughter"

"a **glass of raw milk** may contain milk from **hundreds of cows**"

"some types of *salmonella* can infect a hen's ovary, so the internal contents of **a normal looking egg can be contaminated . . . even before the shell is formed**"

"a **single hamburger** may contain meat from **hundreds of animals**"

"raw foods of animal origin are the **most likely to be contaminated**; that is, **raw meat and poultry, raw eggs, unpasteurized milk, and raw shellfish**"

It's the dose that makes the poison, though. It may not matter if there are a thousand different carcinogens in fast food as long as the dose is so small that you'd have to eat a hundred Big Macs a day to get any sort of toxic dose. So the exact levels in each item were measured. According to the EPA, the maximum tolerable exposure to dioxins for children is 120 femtograms a day—that's less than one-trillionth of the weight of a paperclip. This makes dioxins one of the most toxic substances known to humankind. So, less than 120 for the entire day is the safety window for our kids.

How much dioxin is there in a Big Mac? Maybe 50 femtograms,

we wouldn't let our kids play in a field with a chemical-spewing cropduster flying overhead, but when that "airplane" flies into their mouths with a spoonful of this or a forkful of that, what are we exposing them to?

staples on too many school lunch menus, like hamburgers, ice cream, and cheese pizza, come loaded with DDT, dioxins, and PCBs. as if that weren't shocking enough, these other faves have their own grisly ingredients.

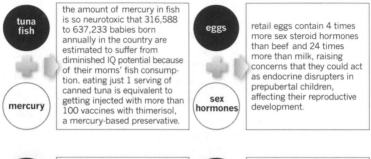

tuna fish ➜ **mercury**

the amount of mercury in fish is so neurotoxic that 316,588 to 637,233 babies born annually in the country are estimated to suffer from diminished IQ potential because of their moms' fish consumption. eating just 1 serving of canned tuna is equivalent to getting injected with more than 100 vaccines with thimerisol, a mercury-based preservative.

eggs ➜ **sex hormones**

retail eggs contain 4 times more sex steroid hormones than beef and 24 times more than milk, raising concerns that they could act as endocrine disrupters in prepubertal children, affecting their reproductive development.

chicken "fingers" ➜ **arsenic**

when we eat chickens, in addition to DDT, dioxins, and PCBs, we're also ingesting arsenic. these birds are fed arsenic-containing compounds to boost their growth (i.e., to reach slaughter faster and bigger) by helping to wipe out some of the parasite load, which results from their overcrowded conditions on factory farms.

hotdogs ➜ **carcinogens**

carcinogenic nitrosamines, formed by the cooking of meats cured with sodium nitrite to maintain the bloody red color, may be the reason that children eating 3 or more hotdogs a week appear to have twice the odds of developing brain tumors and 10 times the odds of developing childhood leukemia.

almost half a child's daily dioxin allowance in a single burger? A single slice of pizza? One drumstick or a single scoop of ice cream? Maybe even 100? No. According to the best data available, a Big Mac rivals one scoop of ice cream at not 100 femtograms or even 200, but at as many as 49,000 femtograms—that's 400 times the maximum tolerable dose of dioxins in every scoop and every burger. It's even worse if parents take their children out for pizza or KFC, where they may be exposing their children to almost 1,000 times the maximum tolerable dose of toxic waste.

In the end, how we raise Leo goes beyond merely following our ethical compasses or simply ensuring as best we can that our son is healthy. Our choices for him and the decisions we hope he will make as he matures are for all of us—ourselves, the planet, and nonhuman animals. That's the most important lesson we hope to pass on to our son—that we can make a difference at every single meal.

> "Kindness and compassion towards all living things is a mark of a civilized society. Conversely, cruelty, whether it is directed against human beings or against animals, is not the exclusive province of any one culture or community of people."
>
> —Cesar Chavez

7

Workers

Christine Chavez and Julie Chavez Rodriguez

These words by our grandfather Cesar Chavez were written on December 26, 1990. Today, nearly two decades later, we are still fighting the same struggles on behalf of humans and animals.

The individuals who toil in factory farms and slaughterhouses engage in some of the most dangerous work in the nation to put meat, eggs, and dairy products on our tables. Their wages and treatment by employers often do not reflect the severe and sometimes fatal occupational hazards they face every day. Many factory farm workers and slaughterhouse employees are also immigrants who may be undocumented or have difficulty with the English language, putting them in a precarious position when it comes to unionizing, reporting workplace injuries, or simply having an opportunity to work in the United States.

As the United Nations has noted, the three most dangerous industries in the world are mining, construction, and agriculture. Occupational hazards for agricultural workers include the use of dangerous machinery and exposure to toxic pesticides and diseases that are transmissible from farm animals.

Factory farm workers typically receive low salaries despite their

Christine Chavez works on campaigns to advance progressive causes. For eight years, she served as the political director of the United Farm Workers Union. Julie Chavez Rodriguez is currently the programs director for the Cesar E. Chavez Foundation.

the shit pit

who
workers

why
noxious gases including hydrogen sulfide, methane, and ammonia, dust, and harmful bacteria generated by decomposing manure that can cause toxic, oxygen-deficient, and/or explosive atmospheres and respiratory problems, including asthma, bronchitis, acute respiratory distress syndrome, and organic dust toxic syndrome, in 1 in 4 workers

what
massive pits storing the overwhelming amount of manure produced by factory-farmed animals in which workers can—and do—die from asphyxiation, succumbing to toxic gases, and attempting to rescue others

when
fatalities frequent enough for the national institute for occupational safety and health to issue such publications as "preventing deaths of farm workers in manure pits" and "niosh warns: manure pits continue to claim lives"

where
underground or, in the case of egg factory farms, on the ground-floor of a warehouse-like shed

long hours and occupational health risks. The chief source of these health hazards is the collection and disposal of waste produced by the vast numbers of animals confined in a single facility. For example, the method of collecting manure that is typical of dairy and pig factory farms is the use of underground manure storage pits or outdoor manure "lagoons," the latter having the capacity to hold as much as 20 to 45 million gallons of waste.

Decomposing manure generates noxious gases such as hydrogen sulfide, methane, and ammonia, as well as dust and harmful bacteria. Hydrogen sulfide, which can build up to toxic levels in underground manure storage pits, has been deemed "a leading cause of sudden death in the workplace" by the National In-

"Numerous studies document serious respiratory problems among CAFO workers, including chronic bronchitis and non-allergic asthma in about 25 percent of confinement swine workers. Workers exposed to the potent neurotoxin hydrogen sulfide at levels only slightly higher than those at which its odor becomes detectable (5.0 ppm vs .025 ppm), have been found to have accelerated deterioration of neurobehavioral function; and [s]cientists convened first by the Centers for Disease Control and Prevention (CDC), and more recently by the University of Iowa and Iowa State University, agree CAFO air emissions may constitute a hazard to public health, in addition to workers' health."[22]

— Excerpted from the American Public Health Association's Precautionary Moratorium on New Concentrated Animal Feed Operations

---

stitute for Occupational Safety and Health (NIOSH). As the Farm Safety Association has also observed: "Since the increased use of manure storage facilities in agriculture there have been numerous instances where a farmer, family member, or employee has asphyxiated or succumbed to toxic gases from the storage. Cases have been documented where several individuals have died while attempting to rescue a coworker or family member from an underground pit or a spreader tank."

A number of NIOSH reports document worker fatalities caused by exposure to the chemicals in manure pits. The agency even issued an alert in 1990 entitled *Preventing Deaths of Farm Workers*

bringing home (more than) the bacon

workers in "typical" factory farms "where animals are densely confined" are subjected to "dusts from the animals, their feed, and their feces, ammonia. . .and hydrogen sulfide, which can be hazardous" to their health. **below are prevalence rates of symptoms endured by pig factory workers.**

symptom	prevalence
cough	67%
sputum or phlegm	56%
scratchy throat	54%
runny nose	45%
burning or watering eyes	39%
headaches	37%
tightness of chest	36%
shortness of breath	30%
wheezing	27%
muscle aches and pains	25%

in Manure Pits, which covers the harmful effects of the chemicals commonly found in these holding tanks.

Numerous studies have also documented such respiratory problems among factory farm workers as impaired respiratory function, chronic bronchitis, occupational asthma, and organic dust syndrome. As many as 70 percent of factory farm workers suffer from acute bronchitis and 25 percent develop chronic bronchitis.

Indeed, *New Yorker* writer Michael Specter said of his first visit to a chicken farm: "I was almost knocked to the ground by the overpowering smell of feces and ammonia. My eyes burned and so did my lungs, and I could neither see nor breathe. . . . There must

Nearly every worker interviewed for this report bore physical signs of a serious injury suffered from working in a meat or poultry plant. Their accounts of life in the factories graphically explain those injuries. Automated lines carrying dead animals and their parts for disassembly move too fast for worker safety. Repeating thousands of cutting motions during each work shift puts enormous traumatic stress on workers' hands, wrists, arms, shoulders and backs. They often work in close quarters creating additional dangers for themselves and coworkers. They often receive little training and are not always given the safety equipment they need. They are often forced to work long overtime hours under pain of dismissal if they refuse.[23]

A special investigative report in 2003 by the *Omaha World-Herald* documented death, lost limbs, and other serious injuries in Nebraska meatpacking industry plants since 1999. Much of the evidence involved night shift cleaners, most of them undocumented workers. OSHA documents dryly recorded what happened:

- "Cleaner killed when hog-splitting saw is activated."
- "Cleaner dies when he is pulled into a conveyer and crushed."
- "Cleaner loses legs when a worker activates the grinder in which he is standing."

- "Cleaner loses hand when he reaches under a boning table to hose meat from chain."
- "Hand crushed in rollers when worker tries to catch a scrubbing pad that he dropped."

In all, the report concluded, nearly one hundred night shift cleaning workers in the state meatpacking industry suffered amputations and crushings of body parts in the period (1999–2003) reviewed by the investigative team. These severe injuries are just the tip of an iceberg of thousands of lacerations, contusions, burns, fractures, punctures, and other forms of what the medical profession calls traumatic injuries, distinct from the endemic phenomenon in the industry of repetitive stress or musculoskeletal injury.[24]

Meatpackers try to maximize the volume of animals that go through the plant by increasing the speed at which animals are processed. The speed of the processing line is thus directly related to profits. However, the fact that line speed is also directly related to injuries has not prompted federal or state regulators to set line speed standards based on health and safety considerations.

The sheer volume and speed of slaughtering operations in the meat and poultry industry create enormous danger. Workers labor amid

high-speed automated machinery moving chickens and carcasses past them at a hard-to-imagine velocity: four hundred head of beef per hour, one thousand hogs per hour, thousands of broilers per hour, all the time workers pulling and cutting with sharp hooks, knives, and other implements. Meat and poultry workers interviewed by Human Rights Watch and by other researchers consistently cite the speed of the lines as the main source of danger. "The chain goes so fast that it doesn't give the animals enough time to die," said one beef plant worker.[25]

---

have been thirty thousand chickens sitting silently on the floor in front of me. They didn't move, didn't cluck. They were almost like statues of chickens, living in nearly total darkness, and they would spend every minute of their six-week lives that way."

Due to the many health risks posed to both workers and neighbors of factory farms, the American Public Health Association has called for a moratorium on the construction of new factory farms.

Factory farms are notoriously understaffed, with underpaid workers being tasked with unachievable responsibilities. Said one undercover investigator employed at a massive egg production facility: "Each worker here is responsible for monitoring between 120,000 to 170,000 hens every day. Even if we had no other duties, it would be impossible to check on each bird or even thoroughly look inside each cage. . . . [T]here are so many mechanical problems (primarily with the egg collection system) to attend to that there is even less time to look after the birds. I try to spend as much time as possible looking for birds stuck in the wires of their cages

dying to work					
occupation	annual average employment	no. of occupational injuries*	rate of occupational injuries	no. of occupational fatalities	rate of occupational fatalities
raising and slaughtering animals in the meat, egg, and milk industries	618,400	44,600	1 in 14 workers	150	1 in 4,123 workers
highway, street, and bridge construction	347,000	19,500	1 in 18 workers	95	1 in 3,691 workers
roofing	205,000	10,800	1 in 19 workers	94	1 in 2,158 workers
coal mining	205,000	4,200	1 in 18 workers	27	1 in 2,867 workers
logging	61,600	2,900	1 in 21 workers	88	1 in 700 workers

and removing dead birds from cages with live hens, but there simply is not enough time in the day."

The frustrations and dangers faced by factory farm workers are rivaled by those endured by slaughterhouse workers. The work environment in slaughterhouses poses "risks greater than those faced by workers in many other manufacturing operations," according to the U.S. Government Accountability Office. Human Rights Watch characterizes slaughterhouse jobs as "the most dangerous factory jobs in the country." A report about slaughterhouse workers prepared by the organization states that "[a]lmost every worker interviewed . . . began with the story of a serious injury he or she suffered in a meat or poultry plant, injuries reflected in their scars, swellings, rashes, amputations, blindness, or other afflictions."

Slaughterhouse work causes high rates of injury and musculoskeletal disorders such as repetitive stress injuries, and may even result in death. Exacerbating these problems are insufficient training, long hours, cutting animals in close quarters, and fast line speeds. The troublesome situation in which workers may find themselves following an injury is compounded by the fact that em-

> In an interview with author Donald Stull, "Peggy," who worked on the "presenting and trimming" line at a chicken slaughter plant, said: "There is no bathroom break. You do not leave that line. They will relieve you to go to the bathroom, but you get in trouble for it. They say you don't, but you do . . . because you do those chickens or USDA shuts the line down."[26]

ployers often withhold compensation by denying that the injury was indeed work-related.

The Congressional Research Service reports that line speeds have been a consistent complaint among slaughterhouse workers for over a century. At the world's largest pig processing plant, owned by Smithfield Foods, approximately 5,000 workers a day labor "on a maze of assembly lines that herd, pull, split, slice, de-bone, de-fat and otherwise dismember hogs at a rate of up to 32,000 a day, 2,000 an hour, 33 a minute, or one hog every two seconds."

Direct contact with animals who are still alive is one aspect of animal slaughter that threatens worker safety: those who "are still dying when they are hung on the line . . . may struggle and thrash about wildly." In poultry slaughterhouses, workers face the additional hazard of birds who begin their journey down the slaughter line by being shackled upside down while still conscious, a process referred to as "live hang."

Birds comprise the majority of animals slaughtered in the United States, amounting to more than nine billion birds annually. Ironically, the protections of the federal Humane Methods of Slaughter Act are not extended to these animals. As a result, poultry slaughterhouses are not required to render them unconscious before they are hung upside-down in shackles.

Live-hang workers thus have the "laborious, unpleasant and hazardous job" of "constantly and rapidly lift[ing] bunches of chickens . . . to overhead hooks to begin the slaughtering and dis-assembly process." Some of the hazards this creates for workers are caused by inadequate lighting, too-fast line speeds, and poor ergonomics. Many of the dangers created by live hanging result from workers having to turn still-conscious birds upside down and shackle them on an overhead conveyor line. The birds' reactions include scratching, pecking, biting, urinating, and defecating on workers.

While many workplace injuries go unreported, in 2004 almost 20,000 poultry slaughterhouse workers reported occupational illnesses or injuries severe enough to warrant missing work or seeking medical care. The poultry processing industry had the sixth-highest rate of occupational illness and injury of any private industry that year. Researchers at Wake Forest University School of Medicine have also found that rates for carpal tunnel syndrome and similar medical conditions have been on the rise among poul-try slaughterhouse workers despite their decline among workers in other manufacturing industries.

In a letter to KFC, former slaughterhouse worker Virgil Butler wrote: "I worked at the Tyson plant in Grannis, Arkansas, from July, 1997, until November 12, 2002. I worked on the night shift in the Receiving department as a live-hanger as well as on the kill-floor. I personally witnessed many acts of cruelty toward the chickens by employees of the plant on a nightly basis. . . . We were extremely shorthanded, due to the horrendous working conditions. This led to a high turnover rate with inexperienced, frustrated, workers un-der pressure to keep the production numbers up. If production fell, it would mean overtime work, so the belt speed was turned up. This resulted in the belt becoming overloaded in the area where the chickens awaited shackling, which ended up smothering hundreds of chickens a night ... These uncomfortable conditions, coupled with the unrelenting pressure to keep the shackles filled at all costs, lead to much frustration and outright rage among the employees."

Many factory farm and slaughterhouse workers are immigrants. For example, in Arkansas, one of the nation's leading broiler (meat-type) chicken producers, the immigrant population almost tripled during the 1990s from 25,000 to 74,000. Most of these individuals labor in the state's meat and poultry processing plants.

Compared to workers born in the United States, immigrant workers are more likely to have difficulties with the English language and lack an awareness of applicable laws. This can prevent them from knowing about their rights or the hazards of the work they are undertaking.

Many of these workers are also undocumented. Reasonably fearing the consequences should authorities become aware of their immigration status, these workers are less likely to organize to improve conditions or even seek protection for their rights.

A 2002 decision by the Supreme Court made matters even worse for undocumented workers. As a result of the Court's decision, employers who illegally fire undocumented workers for union organizing activities that are protected under the National Labor Relations Act are not required to pay them back wages.

The employment of undocumented workers can also create problems for their U.S.-born colleagues. An employee of a Pilgrim's Pride poultry processing plant in Alabama has filed a class action suit against the company alleging that the plant's management hired undocumented workers with the intention of reducing wages for all the plant's employees.

In addition to the consequences for undocumented workers outlined above, other slaughterhouse workers have also been unjustly denied the opportunity to seek better working conditions or to organize. According to one poultry slaughterhouse worker, his employer "always gets rid of workers who protest or who speak up for others. When they jumped [the line speed] from thirty-two chickens a minute to forty-two, a lot of people protested. The company came right out and asked who the leaders were. Then they fired them."

Perhaps the most high-profile attempt to organize is the ongoing battle between workers at a pig processing plant in Tar Heel, North Carolina, and Smithfield Foods, the company that owns and operates the plant. Working with these individuals, the United Food and Commercial Workers Union (UFCW) has called attention to their struggle with its "Justice at Smithfield" campaign.

According to Human Rights Watch, the laundry list of offenses committed by the company includes threatening to: fire union supporters and to close the plant if workers chose union representation, call immigration authorities to report immigrant workers if workers chose union representation, use violence against workers engaged in organizing activities, and blacklist workers who support the union. Furthermore, the plant's management has disciplined, suspended, and fired workers because of their support for the union and has spied on workers engaged in lawful union activities.

Former Senator John Edwards recently sent a letter to the president of Smithfield Foods, which calls on the company to protect the rights of workers at its Tar Heel plant and to stay out of their unionizing efforts. Edwards wrote: "Protecting the right to organize in our democracy is important because it allows working men and women to help make decisions that affect their work lives. I hope and expect that you will protect the right of your workers in North Carolina and across the country to form a union and bargain collectively."

One of the many aspects of modern food production that is

never included on package labeling is the treatment of the people whose labor produced it. To truly stand up for those who are silenced, mistreated, harassed, intimidated, sickened, injured, and sometimes killed in factory farms and slaughterhouses is to look at their suffering as an ingredient in most of the meat, egg, and dairy products that line our supermarket shelves. No matter how cheap the price tag may be, it is not worth participating in the systematic exploitation of the nation's factory farm and slaughterhouse workers.

We would all benefit by remembering Cesar Chavez's simple, yet eloquent words: "Only when we have become nonviolent towards all life will we have learned to live well with others."

"[T]he vast majority of America's meat and produce are controlled by a handful of ruthless monopolies that house animals in industrial warehouses where they are treated with unspeakable and unnecessary cruelty. These meat factories destroy family farms and rural communities and produce vast amounts of dangerous pollutants that are contaminating America's most treasured landscapes and waterways." [27]

—Robert F. Kennedy Jr.

"I could be out in the gardens, and you have to run for the house if the wind switches direction."

—Herb Guth, Peoria County, Illinois

"People want to talk about the smell—that it is unpleasant. The smell is a warning, the particulate matter that is being emitted and embedded into your lungs is much more serious. As a group, we are concerned, gravely concerned. Not just for ourselves, but for all of the people in this community now, and all those who will come after us."

—Jay Coffman, Rush County, Indiana

8

Communities

Paul and Phyllis Willis

The individuals in the preceding quotes, and thousands like us across the country, bear many of the costs associated with industrial meat, egg, and dairy production. Factory farms, also known as concentrated animal feeding operations (CAFOs), have become the dominant way of raising farm animals in the United States.

Phyllis and I have been farming since 1976. We started raising pigs when a neighbor called me and said he had a sow with five pigs and he would sell me the sow and give me the pigs. Within a year, I had ten female pigs. I borrowed a boar from a neighbor, and four months later we had seventy piglets. We continued expanding our herd and accumulating outdoor huts and started raising pigs on pasture in a natural system much the way I had learned as a boy working with my father. My job back then was to ride my bicycle to the field and check on the pigs twice a day.

Fast forward to today. We now have over 500 farmers in the Niman Ranch Pork Company, and Phyllis and I have had visitors from all over the world just because we are raising pigs the right way and not producing protein units in a pollution factory.

Industrial factory farms tend to cluster in regions where input costs are lower and environmental regulations are more lenient;

Paul Willis serves as the manager of Niman Ranch Pork Company and is the owner and operator of the Willis Free Range Pig Farm in Thornton, Iowa. Phyllis Willis is a community activist.

location, location, location

in addition to greater health risks, what else may you expect if a factory farm
moves into your community?

**lower property values, family income,
retail sales, quality of life, and farm
worker wages**

**higher rates of poverty, tension, anger,
depression, fatigue, and confusion**

it should be no surprise, then, that in rural iowa, which leads the united states
in both egg and pig production, a survey found that **the development of a
factory farm was equally or less desirable than the construction of prisons,
solid-waste landfills, slaughter plants, and sewage treatment plants.**

North Carolina and Iowa are frequently cited examples of geographic concentration. Two decades ago, North Carolina produced
2.6 million pigs per year. It now produces 10 million pigs and generates around 19 million tons of pig waste annually. In our state
of Iowa, in just two decades, we've seen an 84 percent decrease
in the number of farms that raise pigs in the state, while the average number of pigs per farm escalated from 250 to 1,430, nearly a
sixfold increase.

What does this mean for the communities where these farms are
located? How do factory farms assault communities and quality of
life in rural America?

As discussed extensively in chapters 2 and 5, factory farms contribute to land, water, and air pollution and have also been impli-
cated in climate change. Aside from these forms of environmental

"One of the most important issues confronting agricultural communities in the United States—perhaps the most important issue—is the future structure of the livestock industry. The issue is whether animals will be raised on diversified, sustainable family farms or produced in large, energy- and capital-intensive confinement facilities such as factory farms that concentrate the animals and their wastes in vast quantities and concentrate economic control in the hands of absentee investors. At stake is the prosperity and health of rural communities, access to economic opportunity for farm and rural families, the future of this country's rural environment and far-reaching questions of food safety and affordability. Family farmers and other rural residents are upset, angry and fighting back as factory farms pollute air, water and soil; uproot social structures; drive farmers out of business; and threaten the quality of life." [28]
—Brad Trom in *The Grand Forks Herald*

degradation, however, animal factories deteriorate our health, dismantle our quality of life, and devalue our properties.

The U.S. Department of Agriculture reports that approximately 500 million tons of manure are produced by confined farm animals every year. Based on this figure, the U.S. Environmental Protection Agency estimates that "all confined animals generate 3 times more raw waste than is generated by humans in the U.S." Such massive amounts of manure and the byproducts contained in the waste, including heavy metals, pathogen bacteria, and volatile gases, are so damning to the health of factory farm workers and neighboring communities that the largest association of public health professionals, the American Public Health Association, resolved in 2003 to urge federal, state, and local governments and public health agencies to impose a moratorium on the construction of new factory farms.

Studies abound demonstrating the health risks of living near these animal factories. A 2002 report released by Iowa State University and the University of Iowa found that hydrogen sulfide and ammonia emissions from factory farms can pose a health risk to humans. In North Carolina, researchers have compared physical health symptoms of residents in three communities—two near factory farms confining either pigs or cattle and one in another rural area without any agricultural operations using liquid waste management systems. Residents near the pig factory farm reported more frequent occurrences of "headache, runny nose, sore throat, excessive coughing, diarrhea, and burning eyes." The findings of another study determined that neighbors of a pig factory farm also suffered from respiratory problems, nausea, weakness, and chest tightness. Researchers have also concluded that children attending schools near factory farms suffer elevated levels of asthma symptoms.

Researchers have looked at the effects factory farm odors— produced by decomposing feces, spilled feed, and urine—can have on people living near them. They found that, compared to the control group, individuals living near the factory farm who encountered the odors had "significantly more tension, more depression, more anger, less vigor, more fatigue, and more confusion."

Like many rural Americans, we've lived near pig factory farms and have suffered for it. It is nearly impossible to have any qual-

> "To the Bears, the crisis . . . began . . .
> when the first birds arrived at the new
> Buckeye [egg factory farm] plant behind their
> house. . . . The following February, the ugly
> aspects of living near an egg farm became
> real. Their garage filled with flies eager
> to get into the house, and the air became
> heavy with the stench of chicken manure.
> Their well went down 17 feet, and, in time,
> manure spills signaled the need to test the
> well regularly for bacteria and nitrates. . . .
> During the Bear family reunion on June
> 27, 1999, Rosie passed out fly swatters so
> guests could work on fly control. Robert
> filmed the picnic, panning slowly to show
> flies covering everything in sight—the deck,
> charcoal grill, siding, pant legs, shoes and
> toys. . . . On April 15, 2002, when Rosie was a
> substitute teacher at Marseilles Elementary
> School down the road, she spent the whole
> day fighting flies."
>
> —Excerpted from Fran Henry's article entitled,
>   "State rules still short of ideal, some say," printed
>   on June 2, 2003, in *The Plain Dealer*.

---

ity of life living near these industrial operations. There are manure spills at least every week, leading to fish kills, sometimes for miles down the stream. The air is so foul, people can become sick just while driving by one of these factory farms.

Living in rural communities with farmers who raise animals doesn't have to be like this. We raise pigs on our farm but there is

nightmare neighbors

a scientific study sampler on community health in factory farm-land

increased rates of headaches, eye irritation, chest tightness, respiratory problems, and weakness in pig factory farm neighbors (1)

doubling of production on factory farms could lead to a 7.4% increase in infant mortality, deaths driven by elevated levels of respiratory diseases (2)

higher rates of depression, anger, tension, and fatigue in residents living near factory farms than the control population (3)

elevated rates of respiratory and gastro-intestinal problems, mucous membrane irritation, runny noses, sore throats, excessive coughing, diarrhea, and burning eyes reported for those with factory farm neighbors (4)

12% prevalence of asthma found in a study of 1,000 iowan families, especially among kids on farms raising pigs (44.1%) and raising pigs with antibiotic-laden feed (55.8%) (5)

no stench since we have far fewer animals than a factory farm and don't use manure lagoons. Instead, the animals' manure can be used to fertilize our crops, which will be used to feed them. This is all part of the natural cycle of agriculture that is rapidly being lost at the hands of the corporations that keep building more factory farms.

Neighbors are speaking out around the country—for our health and our quality of life.

Kathleen Neal is part of a group of citizens in South Bend, Indiana, that formed to lobby against a CAFO in their community. In an editorial in the *South Bend Tribune*, she wrote that large-scale animal production facilities are "notorious across the Midwest for

> **"Increased numbers of CAFOs in an area often are associated with declines in local economic and social indicators (e.g., business purchases, infrastructure, property values, population, social cohesion), which undermine the socioeconomic and social foundations of community health, particularly in poor and African American rural communities."** [29]
>
> —Excerpted from the American Public Health Association's Precautionary Moratorium on New Concentrated Animal Feed Operations

the contamination of local water supplies, extremely foul-smelling air, the drying up of local wells and the degradation of local roads and bridges."

In Illinois, Jay Coffman spoke out after a hearing on a 2,000-pig confinement operation that was trying to open in his community: "I suppose some see me as a radical, because I strongly disagree with what is happening to our county. I think that, as a group, we are concerned about serious health issues associated with these individual CAFOs, as well as CAFOs collectively. The hog producers are trying to basically wrap their argument and point of view up in the farming/ag industry, but this is not traditional agriculture. This is industrial agriculture, and there are serious differences."

Willard Jones, a neighbor of a pig factory farm in Alabama, told his local paper, "It's a very unpleasant situation, from the odor and the big black flies and the runoff from the spraying of the fields that gets into the creek and tributary. . . . The water is dark brown to black. It doesn't look healthy at all."

"I am going to talk about water quality and the high levels of bacteria in our water. I am going to speak on behalf of those who still want to go to a creek and go swimming but can't because there is too much *E. coli* in it." These are the words of Dwayne "Bill" Miller, an Arkansas man, as he was preparing to testify at a hearing about the impacts of CAFOs.

Based on the detrimental effects factory farms have on land, water, air, public health, and quality of life in neighboring communities, it is not surprising that they also impact local property values. In fact, studies have shown substantial declines in property values when residences are in close proximity to an industrial animal production facility.

An article in the journal of the Appraisal Institute, an international association of professional real estate appraisers, reports that case studies show that "diminished marketability, loss of use and enjoyment, and loss of exclusivity can result in a diminishment ranging from 50% to nearly 90% of otherwise unimpaired value." Researchers in Pennsylvania found that neighboring house prices drop once the total live weight of confined animals exceeds 200,000 pounds. A study of five counties in north central Iowa determined that nearby residences downwind of a confinement operation may suffer a 10 percent drop in property value.

Neighbors aren't the only ones suffering from factory farms and their industrial practices. Many independent family farms are struggling to survive, unable to compete against these massive operations. It's not uncommon for formerly independent farmers to resort to contractual arrangements with large agribusiness corporations.

Most of these farmers aren't bad people, but they've been sold lies by these corporations, and now there's no getting out. Consumers have also been sold lies about the "benefits" of industrial animal agriculture.

the facts say:
often highly automated and integrated, **industrialized facilities minimize labor**, with workers overseeing hundreds, thousands, or even tens of thousands of animals. **smaller, independent farmers** struggle to compete with large operations and **can lose their jobs and livelihoods**.

they say:
factory farms create jobs, support local businesses, and boost local economies

the facts say:
when a factory farm moves in, property values often fall, draining the tax base and leaving little for higher infrastructure costs. one example: **pig factories in iowa decreased the value of homes within a ½-mile radius by 40% and by 30% for homes within 1 mile.**

the facts say:
large-scale facilities tend to purchase fewer inputs (e.g., building materials, equipment, feed) from local businesses and, compared to smaller farms, **a lesser share of profits from factory farms ends up in local hands, discouraging local economic growth**.

Local farmers contracting with vertically integrated corporations raise animals until slaughter, providing land, buildings, and labor. The corporations supply company-owned animals, feed, and transportation, and the "growers," who typically own the land, must construct company-approved buildings, potentially investing hundreds of thousands of dollars. Karen Charman, an investigative journalist, interviewed Rickey Gray, an assistant to Mississippi's Agriculture Commissioner, about contract growers in 2002. "It's like being a gerbil in a cage, . . ." he said. "All in all, it's like a modern day sharecropping system."

Farmers agree. Royce Johnson, a Texas contract farmer spoke to the *Fort Worth Star-Telegram* in 2005: "They call us 'contract

growers' . . . but they tell us everything we do. If there's just a per-
sonality conflict with your company service tech, you can lose your
contract over that. You can talk to another company, but Tyson
wouldn't sign another farmer that Pilgrim's cut off."

Reports Karen Charman: "Most chicken growers are reluctant
to talk publicly for fear of reprisals. . . . They say the corporations
that control the chicken industry hook new growers on the promise
of making a good, steady income at home. Instead, growers find
themselves trapped in debt-laden relationships that turn them into
serfs at the mercy of the companies that make a fortune on their
backs. . . . Nobody knows how many poultry growers have lost
their contracts because only the companies have that information,
says Mary Clouse, who [formerly ran] . . . the Contract Agriculture/
Poultry Project at the Rural Advancement Foundation International
(RAFI). Poultry companies say the number is very low."

Family farmers are paying a high price—not only financially, but
emotionally as well. Concern over the decline in independent family farms, coupled with the pressures of reduced quality of life and
potential resultant socioeconomic disadvantages when factory
farms move in, can even contribute to CAFO-related posttraumatic
stress disorder symptoms.

In the late 1980s, we started to see more and more pig factory
farms being built in Iowa and North Carolina. It was around that
time that we attended a couple of meetings where representatives
of large agribusiness corporations were pushing the idea that factory farming was the wave of the future. We knew better and so,
rather than follow this trend of industrialization, we continued traditional ways of raising animals, going so far as to invent the term
"free range pigs."

In 1994, I met Bill Niman and began marketing pig to Niman
Schell in San Francisco. This eventually led to a network of farmers
who became the Niman Ranch Pork Co. LLC in 1998, which today

has over 500 members. We're proud of our work with Niman Ranch, which has helped keep hundreds of small, traditional pig farmers in business. We've also been active in regional political battles to decrease the power and presence of factory pig farms in Iowa.

Communities aren't just sitting around—we are organizing against this threat to our welfare. For example, on the East Coast's peninsula where Delaware, Virginia, and Maryland meet, a group of farmers threatened by the contract system, workers facing poor conditions in plants, and neighbors facing agricultural pollution formed the Delmarva Poultry Justice Alliance. Jim Lewis, an Episcopal priest who worked with the group, put it this way, "[W]e have brought together all of the people in the area who have anything to do with a piece of chicken." Working together as a community, the Alliance brought a successful lawsuit against Perdue, Tyson, and three other poultry companies for unpaid overtime wages and helped bring the problems of contract farming to the national stage.

The communities surrounding industrialized meat, egg, and dairy production operations bear the visible damage of factory farming, but the true costs are borne by all of us. We all have a role to play, not just as farmers and neighbors, but as consumers. To quote Wendell Berry, every time each of us makes a decision about food, we are "farming by proxy."

At what point will we all stand together and demand accountability and an end to the devastation caused by factory farming?

"Most and probably all of the distinctive infectious diseases of civilization have been transferred to human populations from animal herds."

—William H. McNeill, *Plagues and Peoples*

A 2009 article in the *American Journal of Preventive Medicine* states: "Given the animal agriculture sector's considerable role in environmental degradation, zoonotic disease emergence, and chronic disease promotion, reducing livestock production and promoting healthy plant-based diets should be a global health priority."[30]

9
Zoonotic Diseases

Michael Greger, M.D.

Eating spinach is a wonderful way to get so many important nutrients for our bodies, but getting *E. coli*—an intestinal bug—from the dark leafy green isn't so wonderful. The *E. coli* didn't come from the spinach, though, since plants don't have intestines. The bacteria came from fecal material, the cause of nearly all food poisoning. People can eat French fries without fear of contracting potato blight because the pathogens that affect plants don't tend to affect us. No one has ever come down with Dutch elm disease. The source of most food poisoning is products of animal origin, with chicken meat being the single most-common cause. Viruses found in fresh meat can even cause "butcher's warts" to erupt from the hands of those who handle fresh poultry, fish, and other meat for a living.

Every year, one in four Americans comes down with food poisoning, all caused by viruses or bacteria that can be destroyed by proper cooking. Unless one treats their kitchen like a biohazard lab, there can be cross-contamination of contagion. In meat-eating households, researchers have found more fecal bacteria in the kitchen—on sponges, dish towels, the sink, and counter surfaces—than they found swabbing the rim of the toilet. We shouldn't have to cook the crap out of our food.

Michael Greger, M.D., is the director of Public Health and Animal Agriculture at the Humane Society of the United States and author of *Bird Flu: A Virus of Our Own Hatching*.

domestication. devastation.

through our domestication and use of animals, devastating human diseases have emerged

who	what	estimated no. of people affected over the last century
sheep and goats	measles	150 million deaths
camels	smallpox	300 million deaths
ducks	human influenza	100 million deaths
pigs	whooping cough	25 million deaths
water buffalos	leprosy	750 million cases
cattle	common cold	75 billion cases
chickens	highly pathogenic avian influenza	300 deaths
great apes (for bushmeat)	HIV/AIDS	25 million deaths
civets	SARS	1,000 deaths

Most of human infectious disease in general originally came from animals, starting 10,000 years ago with their domestication. When we brought animals into the barnyard, they brought their diseases with them.

When we first domesticated ruminants such as sheep and goats, we also domesticated their rinderpest virus, which is thought to have turned into human measles. Now thought of as a relatively benign disease, over the last century measles has killed more than 100 million people worldwide. In a sense, all those deaths can be traced back a few hundred generations to the taming of the first ruminants.

Smallpox likely came from camelpox. We domesticated pigs and got whooping cough, and domesticated ducks and got influenza. Before then, no one likely ever got the flu. Leprosy likely came from water buffalo; the cold virus may have come from cattle. Until domestication, the common cold was only, presumably, common to them.

"During the past decades, many previously unknown human infectious diseases have emerged from animal reservoirs, from agents such as human immunodeficiency virus (HIV), Ebola virus, West Nile virus, Nipah virus and Hanta virus. In fact, more than three quarters of the human diseases that are new, emerging or re-emerging at the beginning of the 21st century are caused by pathogens originating from animals or from products of animal origin."

—World Health Organization, Food and Agriculture Organization of the United Nations, and World Organization for Animal Health (WHO/FAO/OIE). 2004. Report of the WHO/FAO/OIE joint consultation on emerging zoonotic diseases.

By the mid-twentieth century, the "age of infectious disease" was thought to be over. We had penicillin, we had conquered polio, and we had eradicated smallpox. In 1948, the U.S. Secretary of State pronounced that the conquest of all infectious diseases was imminent. Twenty years later, victory was declared by the U.S. Surgeon General: "The war against diseases has been won." Even Nobel Laureates were seduced into the heady optimism. One Nobel-winning virologist wrote in the 1962 text *Natural History of Infectious Disease* that "the most likely forecast about the future of infectious disease is that it will be very dull."

But then something changed. Starting around 1975, after decades of declining infectious disease mortality, the number of Americans dying from infectious diseases started to go back up. Over the last thirty years, more than thirty new diseases have emerged, a rate unprecedented in the history of medicine. If this trend continues, the U.S. Institute of Medicine fears we may soon face a "catastrophic storm of microbial threats."

Medical historians describe this time in which we now live as the "age of the emerging plagues." Never in medical history have so many new diseases appeared in so short a time—and almost all of them have come from animals. Animals were domesticated 10,000 years ago, though. What's changed around the world in recent decades to bring this all upon us?

We have been changing the way animals live.

The leading theory as to the emergence of HIV/AIDS, for example, is "direct exposure to animal blood and secretions as a result of hunting, butchering, or other activities (such as consumption of uncooked contaminated [bush]meat). . . ." The butchering of great apes to feed the workers of the logging industry in west equatorial Africa is the most likely origin of the current AIDS crisis. A chimp was slaughtered a few decades ago and now 25 million people are dead.

At live animal markets in Asia and elsewhere, shoppers can not only pick up still-live animals who are often confined in cramped, stressful, unhygienic conditions, but also viruses like SARS, which spread from these storefront slaughter operations to infect 8,000 people in thirty countries on six continents.

Animal agribusiness took natural herbivores like cows and sheep and turned them into carnivores and cannibals by feeding them slaughterhouse waste, blood, and manure. The meat industry then fed people "downers"—animals too sick even to walk— resulting in the risk of mad cow disease.

Industrial animal agriculture operations feed antibiotics by the truckload to those animals raised and killed for human consumption. An estimated 70 percent of antibiotics in the United States— thousands of tons a year—are fed to farm animals just to promote growth in such stressful and filthy environments. Now there are

> **"Anthropogenic factors such as agricultural expansion and intensification to meet the increasing demand for animal protein, global travel, trade in domestic or exotic animals, urbanization, and habitat destruction comprise some of the major drivers of zoonotic disease emergence."**
>
> —World Health Organization, Food and Agriculture Organization of the United Nations, and World Organization for Animal Health (WHO/FAO/OIE). 2004. Report of the WHO/FAO/OIE joint consultation on emerging zoonotic diseases.

---

multidrug-resistant "superbugs" and we physicians are running out of antibiotics.

Between 1975 and 1995, seventeen food-borne pathogens emerged, including *E. coli* O157:H7 in hamburgers, antibiotic-resistant *Salmonella* in eggs, and urinary tract infection–causing bacteria in chicken meat and pork. The Centers for Disease Control estimates 76 million Americans come down with food-borne illness every year. According to the executive editor of *Meat Processing* magazine, "Nearly every food consumers buy in supermarkets and order in restaurants can be eaten with certainty for its safety— except for meat and poultry products."

In response to the torrent of emerging and reemerging diseases jumping from animals to people, the world's three leading authorities got together in 2004 for a joint consultation: the World Health Organization (WHO), the Food and Agriculture Organization of the United Nations (FAO), and the top veterinary authority in the world, the World Organisation for Animal Health (OIE). They identified four main risk factors for the emergence and spread of these new

"nearly every food consumers buy in supermarkets and order in restaurants can be eaten with certainty for its safety—except for meat and poultry products."

— *meat processing* executive editor

salmonella

"bacterium that is widespread in the intestines of birds, reptiles and mammals"

"can spread to humans via a variety of different foods of animal origin"

"fever, diarrhea and abdominal cramps"

"can invade the bloodstream and cause life-threatening infections"

campylobacter

"these bacteria live in the intestines of healthy birds"

"most raw poultry meat has campylobacter on it"

"causes fever, diarrhea, and abdominal cramps"

"the most commonly identified bacterial cause of diarrheal illness in the world"

"guillain-barre syndrome can be caused by campylobacter infection"

the unholy trinity of pathogens

e. coli 0157:h7

"pathogen that has a reservoir in cattle and other similar animals"

"illness typically follows consumption of food or water...contaminated with...cow feces"

"severe and bloody diarrhea...temporary anemia, profuse bleeding, and kidney failure"

"most common cause of acute kidney failure in children...is caused by infection with *e. coli* 0157:h7 and related bacteria"

diseases. Number one on their list? "Increasing demand for animal protein." Animals were domesticated 10,000 years ago, but never before like this.

Now, with billions of feathered and curly-tailed test tubes for viruses to incubate and mutate within, a WHO official described the last few decades as "the most ambitious short-term experiment in evolution in the history of the world." The dozens of emerging animal disease threats that have characterized this "age of emerging plagues" must be put into perspective. SARS infected thousands and killed hundreds; AIDS has infected millions and kills five peo-

reining in the pale horse

the chief of virology at hong kong's queen mary hospital believes that **"the cause and solution [of the highly pathogenic H5N1 avian influenza virus] lies within the poultry industry."** the diagram below, from the u.s. department of interior's august 2005 report on the bird flu threat, illustrates the **key role domestic poultry play in the development of pandemic influenza.** all influenza viruses start in waterfowl, but there does not seem to be direct spread from the natural duck reservoir directly to mammals or humans; domesticated fowl are required as the stepping stone. the most a wild duck virus seems to be able to do to a person is cause a mild case of pinkeye...**spread wing to wing, the number of chickens killed every day would wrap more than twice around the world's equator.**

—michael greger, m.d., excerpted from <u>bird flu: a virus of our own hatching</u>

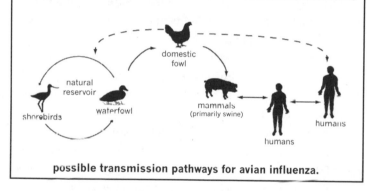

possible transmission pathways for avian influenza.

ple every minute. Only one virus, though, is known to be capable of infecting billions: influenza.

Influenza has been referred to as "last great plague of man," the germ known capable of triggering a global catastrophe. Unlike other devastating infections like malaria, which is largely confined around the equator, or HIV, which is only fluid-borne, influenza is the only virus capable of infecting literally half of humanity in a matter of months. For the 4,500 years since wild birds were first

> **Stefan Pattyn, the editor of *Ebola Virus Haemorrhagic Fever*, wrote: "The larger the scale of man-made environmental changes, the greater must be the probability of emergence of a zoonosis, old or new."**
>
> —Pattyn, S.R., ed. 1978. *Ebola Virus Haemorrhagic Fever.* Amsterdam, The Netherlands: Elsevier North Holland Biomedical Press.

---

domesticated by our ancestors, influenza has always been one of our most contagious infections. Only with the emergence of H5N1 has this virus also emerged as one of our deadliest.

H5N1, the killer strain of avian influenza spreading out of Asia, has so far killed but a handful of people. The reason there is so much concern about bird flu, even in a world in which millions continue to die of diseases like tuberculosis and AIDS, is because the last time a bird flu virus jumped into humans, it triggered the deadliest plague in human history, killing 50 to 100 million people around the globe. Originating from bird flu, the 1918 flu pandemic killed more people in twenty-five weeks than AIDS has killed in twenty-five years. Still, that death toll represents less than 5 percent of the people who were infected with the 1918 flu virus. H5N1 has officially killed nearly two-thirds of its human victims.

Cramming tens of thousands of chickens bred to be almost genetically identical into massive, filthy sheds to stand and lie beak-to-beak in their own waste is a recipe for increasing the virulence and transmission of this virus. "You have to say," concluded virologist Earl Brown, a specialist in the evolution of influenza viruses, "that high-intensity chicken rearing is a perfect environment for generating virulent avian flu virus."

In October 2005, the United Nations issued a press release:

"Governments, local authorities and international agencies need to take a greatly increased role in combating the role of factory-farming . . . [which, combined with live-bird markets] provides ideal conditions for the virus to spread and mutate into a more dangerous form. . . ." The World Health Organization's flu expert in Asia also blamed the emergence of killer viruses like H5N1 in part on intensive animal agriculture and what he called the "[o]verconsumption of animal products." If H5N1 were to mutate into a form easily transmissible from one person to the next, the results could be catastrophic.

Dr. Michael Osterholm is the director of the U.S. Center for Infectious Disease Research and Policy and an associate director within the U.S. Department of Homeland Security. "An influenza pandemic of even moderate impact," he wrote, "will result in the biggest single human disaster ever—far greater than AIDS, 9/11, all wars in the 20th century and the recent tsunami combined. It has the potential to redirect world history as the Black Death redirected European history in the 14th century." For humanity's sake, hopefully the direction world history will take is away from raising billions of birds in intensive confinement to potentially lower the risk of us ever being in this precarious situation ever again.

According to a spokesperson for the World Health Organization, "The bottom line is that humans have to think about how they treat their animals, how they farm them, and how they market them— basically the whole relationship between the animal kingdom and the human kingdom is coming under stress." This recognition of human culpability can offer hope. If our own actions have gotten us into this mess, our future actions may help bring us out.

"Animal welfare is gaining increased recognition as an important element of commercial livestock operations around the world. . . . Animal welfare is just as important to humans for reasons of food security and nutrition. Better management of and care for livestock can improve productivity and food quality, thereby helping to address nutritional deficiencies and food shortages as well as ensuring food safety."[31]

—International Finance Corporation of the World Bank's *Animal Welfare in Livestock Operations* Good Practice Note

10

Global Hunger

Frances Moore Lappé

In 1971, I was a twenty-seven-year-old heretic. With my first book, *Diet for a Small Planet*, the kid from Texas had taken on the cattlemen. I called our grain-fed meat–centered diet the most inefficient, wasteful, irrational system ever devised by humankind. And my greatest heresy? That humans actually thrive without meat. (The cattlemen were so threatened by my radical claim that they quickly set a team of cooks to work to prove *Diet*'s veggie recipes were inedible.)

My own wake-up came in the late 1960s, when all around me experts were sounding the alarm: Global famine was just about upon us, they warned. And its cause? Not enough food! Humanity has simply overrun Earth's capacity.

Could this be? I wanted to know for myself. Burrowing in at the University of California at Berkeley library, I began to unearth the facts and figures only to discover, to my astonishment, that our planet was actually producing *more* than enough calories to feed us all—even to make us chubby. Yet hundreds of millions were going hungry. Today, even more people—now almost a billion—suffer

Frances Moore Lappé is co-founder of Food First, the Institute for Food and Development Policy, and, with her daughter Anna Lappé, of the Small Planet Institute and Small Planet Fund.

no. of gallons of water needed

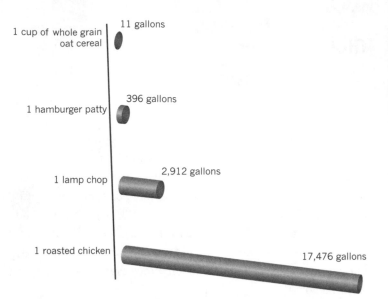

1 cup of whole grain oat cereal — 11 gallons

1 hamburger patty — 396 gallons

1 lamp chop — 2,912 gallons

1 roasted chicken — 17,476 gallons

hunger, even though world food output per person has grown by a fifth since 1980.

In this following-my-nose research, it soon hit me that humans were actively squandering nature's abundance. In the post–World War II era, one-third of the world's grain, along with over 90 percent of soybeans, is going not to humans but is being fed—in a completely new historic twist—to animals in feedlots. And in recent decades, we've even turned a third of our fish catch into feed. Now, roughly one-third of U.S. corn is also transformed into ethanol to feed cars—yet another "perfect solution" for a world in which a billion people are too poor to translate their body's hunger into "market demand" for adequate food.

In *Diet,* I call the cattle feedlot system a "protein factory in reverse." Ruminants, such as cattle, had long served humans by transforming inedible grass into high-grade protein. But today, in the United States, to get just 1 pound of steak on our plate, we funnel 16 pounds of grain and soy into cattle. In addition to all of the other meat-connected assaults on the environment you've read about in these pages, producing that pound also uses enough water to supply a typical American with a daily bath for most of a year.

We humans are actually creating the very scarcity we say we fear. This realization snapped me awake as a young woman. Why? I puzzled. Why would this intelligent species do such a thing?

So I began to explore how the tragedy came to be. As I pondered the post–World War II path to the grain-fed meat-centered diet, it became for me not the problem itself, but a potent *symptom* of the underlying problem: the destructive premise of our entire economy.

The roots of the environmental, health, and animal-welfare travesties linked to factory-farmed meat, eggs, and milk (and detailed in this book) flow inevitably from what I've come to call *one-rule economics*.

And that one rule? Economic decisions driven by highest return to existing wealth—to shareholders and corporate chiefs—all other factors be damned. Driven by this one rule, economic life is ripped from its place within human community, and wealth and power inexorably concentrate. Concentrated wealth then infects and warps political decision-making to serve the interests of the best-off, including giant agribusinesses. Ironically, because it leads to oligopoly, one-rule economics even undermines the open market itself—supposedly the rationale for the whole set up to begin with.

From this rule, the gap separating the world's richest fifth and the world's poorest fifth has doubled in only forty years.

So how does the one-rule economy generate hunger in a world of plenty? To understand, just start with those people who work the

protein conversion (in)efficiencies

according to research by vaclav smil, distinguished professor at the university of manitoba, **dependence on animal products for protein sources is not the most efficient use of resources** in terms of feed efficiency and protein conversion efficiency. funneling grains, including corn and soybeans, through farmed animals for meat and eggs **wastes an overwhelming percentage of protein present in those grains.**

item	wasted protein
beef	**95%** of protein lost
pork	**90%** of protein lost
chicken	**80%** of protein lost
eggs	**70%** of protein lost

land, who are themselves a majority of the hungry. Farmers have virtually no bargaining power in the marketplace of concentration that is inevitable in one-rule economics. They get squeezed on two sides.

First, to buy seeds and machinery, farmers in the Global North have become increasingly dependent on a handful of firms—from Monsanto to John Deere. This model of corporate-dependent farming is now penetrating the Global South. So, farmers in the United States and increasingly many of the billion-plus farmers globally must rely on only a handful of giant suppliers; in effect, they become the "price takers." Similarly, when ready to sell their harvests, farmers face an even more consolidated industry: grain traders and food processors. Here, just three companies control most of the world's grain trade—Cargill, Archer Daniels Midland, and Bunge—and they are the "price makers."

> "Eat less meat. In terms of land use, twenty to one, ten to one . . . most of the food we grow in the world is [used] to feed cattle and pigs, etc. And you know, most of that food actually gets . . . passed through the animal and . . . is not only not good for you; it's an incredibly bad use of land. . . . When I was a graduate student at Berkeley, the second cookbook I bought . . . was . . . called *Diet for a Small Planet* . . . the central thesis was you get an automatically better performance by eating the food yourself instead of feeding it to a cow and then eating the cow. And it's better for you. . . . I still have it on my cookbook shelf. Ah, that was written in the late 60s or mid-60s. It's so true today."[32]
>
> —Steven Chu, U.S. Secretary of Energy and Nobel Laureate

In this squeeze, prices per bushel fall; and farmers then try to survive by eking still *more* from each acre—depressing prices even further. Overall, farm prices have fallen 80 percent in forty years; and the inflation-adjusted world price of corn dropped by more than half between 1980 and 2001. At the same time, the world consumer food price index climbed roughly 350 percent, profiting not farmers but traders, processors, and retailers. Because, as we've noted, desperately poor people throughout the world lack money to make market demand for grain, it makes "economic" sense to feed it to confined animals to produce meat, eggs, and milk—and now fuel—that the better-off will buy.

Thus, in global monopoly capitalism, food isn't food—a source of life. It is another *raw material* to produce something sellable to the better-off—whether it is factory-farmed meat or fuel. Interestingly, as to meat, I use the word "sellable," not "desired," intentionally, for in the 1950s and '60s it took quite an ad campaign and a misleading government grading and labeling system to convince eaters that grain-fed meat—marbled with fat from massive feeding—was desirable.

In one-rule economics, producers are trapped on an endless, single-focused production treadmill, destroying our own and other species' ecological life support. As other chapters show in heartbreaking detail, we generate rural landscapes full of stress and loss—loss of family-scale farms that have proven the world over to be most efficient and loss of diverse species, healthy soil and water, and cared-for animals. None of these staggering losses is, of course, reflected in the price of "cheap grain." No wonder, as this system spreads throughout the world, it fails to end hunger. It intensifies hunger.

So, why think twice about eating factory-farmed meat, eggs, and milk? This book has nine other great reasons. The main impulse of this final reason is the strength the choice gives us. The choice may not change the world, but it does send ripples throughout our economy. Maybe even more importantly, *it changes us*, so we are more able to change the world: as we choose a diet reflecting our body's needs *and* the Earth's, a choice that is aligned with the needs of the most invisible on the planet—small food producers and the hungry worldwide—we feel more aligned inside. (Not to mention healthier!) More aligned, we feel more confidence, more power.

Choosing a plant-and-planet-centered diet is like wearing a string around one's finger. It's a reminder that we have choices. We can choose to live in the real world, not in the make-believe one generated by an economic dogma that destroys life. It's a reminder that this tragedy is needless. It is actively created.

According to a 2007 article in the *European Journal of Clinical Nutrition*, "vegetarian and vegan diets could play an important role in preserving environmental resources and in reducing hunger and malnutrition in poorer nations."[33]

For us, a plant-and-planet-centered diet is a daily reminder that we can re-create economic life so that it reflects our commonsense and deepest values; for, individually, none would *choose* a world that robs farmers of livelihoods, the soil and water of their health, animals and people of their dignity, people of food for their survival. A first step in awakening is to realize that right now, today, we ourselves can begin to make a different choice.

Anna Lappé

When my mother and I arrived on the early morning train into Bhatinda, the heat of the Indian Punjabi state was just starting to kick in. By the peak of the afternoon, the temperature would top 110 degrees.

We were traveling to this sun-baked spot to meet farmers in the heart of the state who have been long viewed as India's granary. These farmers were supposed to be the human evidence of the success of industrial farming. But what we would hear that day—in

---

Anna Lappé is a national bestselling author and acclaimed public speaker on food, sustainability and the environment.

the voices of the dozens of colorfully turbaned Sikh farmers—was anything but success.

Gesturing with intensity, their faces strained, the farmers shared with us stories of falling income and mounting debt, as the world prices for their crops sunk and sunk. We heard about it all: banks foreclosured, exhausted soils, depleted groundwater. And we heard about the epidemic of farmer suicides plaguing the region, part of a staggering nationwide trend of farmer suicides, which have claimed an estimated 150,000 lives in the country from 1997 to 2005.

Their suffering confirmed the logic my mother and her colleagues at the Institute for Food and Development Policy (Food First) laid out in the early 1970s: that increasing yields through input-intensive agriculture in the developing world would not itself end hunger. Without farmers gaining a voice to secure a fairer system, greater production would inevitably drive many farmers off the land, *increasing* their hunger. Furthermore, with the expansion of industrial agriculture, more and more grain, even in the poorest countries, would go to farmed animals or export, not to the hungry. With economic inequality increasing in countries containing 80 percent of the world's people, elites in poor countries can now afford grain-fed meat. And as the taste for factory-farmed meat is sold to populations globally, the burden on the land increases as well: feed-crop production now uses up one-third of all arable land worldwide.

At the end of our stay in India, my mother and I met with a head of India's food distribution system. We told him that in addition to talking with desperate farmers, we had seen football-field-sized hillocks of surplus grain, barely protected from the weather by plastic tarps.

"Oh, yes, we now have the biggest surpluses in history—16 million tons above our 24 million ton buffer stock," he proudly said.

meating demand for food?

according to a united nations environment programme report, *the environmental food crisis*, "stabilizing the current meat production per capita by **reducing meat consumption in the industrialized world and restraining it worldwide** to 2000 levels of 37.4/kg/capita in 2050 would free an estimated 400 million tons of cereal per year for human consumption"—**providing enough cereals to satisfy the annual calorie need for more than 1 billion people in 2050.**

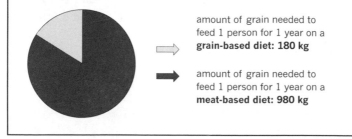

amount of grain needed to feed 1 person for 1 year on a **grain-based diet: 180 kg**

amount of grain needed to feed 1 person for 1 year on a **meat-based diet: 980 kg**

(Not even counting the buffer, that's 32 pounds of grain for every man woman and child in the country.) Since monsoon rains were expected any day, we asked what he planned to do with all this excess.

"We'd like to export it if we can," he said, and we silently mused about exporting to which countries, and for what? To factory farms in China, perhaps, where, like many developing countries, the demand for factory-farmed meat, eggs, and milk has been rapidly increasing? At this rate, the global increase in factory-farmed production will require annual feed consumption of cereals to rise by 292 million metric tons between 1993 and 2020—nearly six times current U.S. grain exports. We also thought of the striking estimate we'd heard that morning from the head of a children's health foundation—that half of India's children suffer from inadequate nutrition.

So we asked what seemed an obvious question: "With so many

hungry people in your country, why don't you just make this surplus available to them?"

The government official looked at us as if we suggested he donate the Parliament building to the homeless. "Oh no, we couldn't do that," he said. "We already give too many subsidies to the poor."

Now, when we hear someone claiming that hunger could be wiped out if we only figured out how to produce more food—more genetic modification! more chemical fertilizers!—we picture the mountains of surplus we saw, and their fate to feed not hungry mouths, but possibly farmed animals half a world away.

Epilogue

Miyun Park

I've never been much of a conspiracy theorist, as much as I love to hear about a juicy set of seemingly unrelated happenstances lead- ing to an alarming series of jaw-dropping consequences. That said, it's hard not to think about conspiracies when you look at the facts. The impacts. Of industrial animal agriculture.

The disturbing reality, though, is that there isn't a conspiracy. There isn't a single mastermind or a single secret club that controls animal agribusiness and has orchestrated its relative impunity. We've all been involved. We've all been enablers or, even worse, granted authority every time we've supported them. But, with that culpability comes empowerment. If we allowed this to happen, we can stop it.

I've tried to write this epilogue twenty-three times. Really. Each time, I've felt utterly inadequate to effectively and poignantly syn- thesize and analyze all of the information painstakingly detailed in these ten short essays. How do I write the last piece for this collec- tion in a way that will inspire, engage, motivate, anger, and support each one of us to yell in a vein-popping way, *"Enough!"*?

Maybe I don't need to feel all of that pressure because maybe the facts speak for themselves; and maybe none of us needs some profound conclusion, because maybe the "the end" to this story is actually the foreword and we find ourselves plopped into the mid- dle of the drama, not only poised, but crouched, to act and react.

Each one of the amazing contributors to this book has her and his story about why it matters enough to speak out. My own starts

Miyun Park is the executive director of Global Animal Partnership.

with a tote bag. I wanted a free one, and an environmental group was offering a pretty great one as a gift if you donated $10 to save the pandas. Who doesn't love pandas? So, I sent in a check to make a difference, and though I never got the free tote, an animal advocacy organization got my name and address and sent me mail about the way animals are raised and killed for my breakfast, lunch, and dinner. I not only didn't know, but I didn't want to know. I had been more than willing not to think about farmed animals and had done so very effectively for the first nineteen years of my little life. But, you can't unknow something. And once you do know, you can't not do something.

And that's how I met Moby. He couldn't not do something either, so he contacted us, wanting to know what, if anything, he could do to help us help farmed animals. Like me, he's concerned about the plight of all animals, human and nonhuman, but, like me, he chooses to focus on the suffering of those raised for food, given the staggering numbers of them who are "produced" and "processed" around the clock and around the world.

So, I found myself on my way to Manhattan, increasingly nervous. I mean, he's Moby, right?

Within the first three or so minutes, I realized I had worked myself into a self-deprecating frenzy for nothing. As much as I wanted him to work with us, he wanted us to want to work with him. And after another ten or so minutes, I realized that although I didn't know him, I did, if that makes sense. We share the same inappropriate sense of humor. The same unwillingness to be quiet when we see something's unjust. And the same priority: to do whatever we're able to do about the unconscionable, irresponsible, and completely depressing practices of the factory farming industry.

When he asked me if I wanted to work with him on this book project, I obviously got excited—not only because it was a creative and hopefully effective way to help make things a little better, but because we got to collaborate with some of the most incredible advocates I've had the fortune to know.

This book isn't about veganism and it isn't about bringing down the animal agriculture industry. It's about social justice and ethics and, not to sound melodramatic, the truth. These things are happening, whether we realize it or not. And these things are negatively impacting too many sectors. Too many issues. Too many movements. Too many individuals. Which is why this eclectic group of people—a pig farmer and his community activist wife, a mother and her daughter, a corporate CEO and a nonprofit CEO, a medical doctor, a shoe store owner and her editor husband, a champion athlete, two cousins born into the workers' rights movement, two climate change activists, a model and designer related to former President George W. Bush, a musician, and me—have gotten together.

We have laws that tell us we can't sell artificially colored potatoes in Alabama, mock contestants in a boxing match if we're spectators in Louisiana, own more than six (ahem) dildos or artificial vaginas in Texas, make fun of someone who doesn't accept a challenge in West Virginia, and go out in public if we have a sniffly cold in Washington state, but there are no laws that tell us we can't mutilate—castrate, de-toe, de-beak, de-horn, and then some—farmed animals without providing anesthesia or analgesia. No laws telling us that we can't confine nursing pigs so restrictively they can't even turn around, can't force chickens and turkeys to grow so fast and so huge that their bodies struggle to survive, and can't "inhumanely" slaughter billions of farmed birds and fish every year. As if that weren't absurd and offensive enough, somehow industrial animal agribusiness has largely managed to get away with oppressing workers, making us and our children unhealthy, slowly but surely destroying rural communities, contributing to global warming and global hunger, cultivating the emergence of devastating zoonotic diseases, and polluting the water we drink, the air we breathe, and the land on which we all live—all while getting subsidized by taxpayers.

And that's why we're here. At the end of the story, which is really just the beginning. Enough. We can't let this continue and we won't, because, really, could it get worse? Could it be more destructive? Could it hurt the collective "us" more? No. It's as bad as we'll let it get. Enough.

Thank you in advance,
Miyun
Washington D.C., 2009

About the Contributors

Brendan Brazier, two-time Canadian 50km Ultra Marathon Champion, raced Ironman triathlons professionally for seven years before becoming a bestselling author on performance nutrition (*The Thrive Diet*, Penguin, 2007) and the creator of Vega (http://sequelnaturals.com/vega), an award-winning line of whole-food nutritional products. He is one of only a few professional athletes in the world whose diet is 100 percent plant based. Named one of the "25 Most Fascinating Vegetarians" by *VegNews* magazine and one of the "Top 40 under 40" by *Natural Food Merchandiser*, Brendan has lectured on the role that food plays—in our health and that of the environment—throughout North America (www.brendan brazier.com).

Lauren Bush is the chief executive officer and co-founder of FEED Projects (www.feedprojects.org), a charitable company with the mission of creating good products that help feed the world. Each FEED bag sold provides hungry children with school meals through the United Nations' World Food Program (WFP). Lauren has been an Honorary Spokesperson for WFP since 2003, and has traveled to Guatemala, Cambodia, Lesotho, Sri Lanka, Chad, Tanzania, Rwanda, and Honduras to help in the fight against hunger and created the initial FEED 1 bag. As a model, Lauren has carved her own niche in the fashion world and was featured on the cover of various publications such as *Vogue*, *Vanity Fair*, *Glamour*, *Tatler*, *W*, and *Town and Country*. She now resides in New York City, where she works on FEED and other socially conscious and eco-friendly projects, such as a women's wear line she designed called Lauren Pierce, which utilizes environmentally friendly and worldly fabrics.

Christine Chavez once heard her grandfather Cesar Chavez say, "We don't need perfect political systems. We need perfect participation." Taking his words to heart, she has come to master the art of modern-day campaigning and community organizing. For eight years, she served as the political director of the United Farm Workers Union (www.ufw.org), the organization her grandfather helped co-found in 1962, and during her tenure, was named by *Latina Magazine* as one of the top Latinas for her longtime involvement with civil rights issues. Today, she works on campaigns to advance progressive causes, putting to use her years of experience with farm workers to level the playing field for issues she believes in. Lauded by such organizations as the Chicana Latina Foundation of San Francisco and the Rhode Island Women's Fund, and recently profiled in *Oprah* magazine for her involvement in the Gen 2 Project, Christine's work—and her compassion for animals—are based on the values passed down to her from her grandfather: the fight for civil rights, social justice, and labor equality.

Michael Greger, M.D., is Director of Public Health and Animal Agriculture at Humane Society International (www.humanesociety.org). An internationally recognized lecturer, he has presented at the Conference on World Affairs, the National Institutes of Health, and the International Bird Flu Summit, among countless other symposia and institutions, testified before U.S. Congress, and was invited as an expert witness in defense of Oprah Winfrey at the infamous "meat defamation" trial. Among his recent publications are articles in *Critical Reviews in Microbiology*, *International Journal of Food Safety Nutrition and Public Health*, *American Journal of Preventive Medicine*, and *Biosecurity and Bioterrorism*, exploring the public health implications of industrialized animal agriculture. His latest book, *Bird Flu: A Virus of Our Own Hatching*, is available full-text at no cost at www.BirdFluBook.org. Dr. Greger is a graduate of the Cornell University School of Agriculture and the Tufts University School of Medicine.

Sara Kubersky, Tom O'Hagan, and their son Leo are native New Yorkers and longtime advocates for reducing suffering. Sara, with her sister Erica, is the co-owner of MooShoes (www.mooshoes.com), a cruelty-free shoe store established in 2001 in Manhattan. Originally located in a defunct butcher shop, MooShoes currently operates in New York City's Lower East

Side and provides increasing numbers of caring consumers from around the world with animal-friendly footwear and information on factory farming practices. Tom, who works in product development for a publishing/information resource company and formerly co-owned Chainsaw Safety Records, an independent label based in Queens, has written about music in such outlets as *Rumpshaker* fanzine and *Rockpile* magazine, and currently blogs about film, books, and music. Their son Leo, who has been vegan for his entire life, is the embodiment of how healthy an animal product–free diet can be.

Anna Lappé is a national bestselling author and public speaker on food, sustainability, and the environment. Named one of *Time*'s Eco–Who's Who, Lappé has been featured in the *New York Times*, *Gourmet*, and *Food & Wine* and appears regularly as an expert commentator on television and radio. From 2004 to 2006, Anna was a Food and Society Policy Fellow with the Kellogg Foundation and serves on the board of directors for Rainforest Action Network. The co-author of *Hope's Edge and Grub*, Anna's third book, *Eat the Sky: Food, Farming, and Climate Change* will be published by Bloomsbury in 2010. She, along with Frances Moore Lappé, is a co-founder of the Small Planet Institute (www.smallplanet.org) and Small Planet Fund (www.smallplanetfund.org).

Frances Moore Lappé is the author of sixteen books, from *Diet for a Small Planet* in 1971 to *Getting a Grip: Clarity, Creativity, and Courage in a World Gone Mad* in 2007. Both were recommended as must-reads for the next president in a 2008 *New York Times Book Review* feature. She is co-founder of Food First, the Institute for Food and Development Policy; and, with her daughter Anna Lappé, of the Small Planet Institute (www.smallplanet.org) and Small Planet Fund. (www.smallplanetfund.org). *Gourmet* magazine chose her as among "25 People Who Changed Food in America," and in 2008 she was named the James Beard Foundation's Humanitarian of the Year. In 1987 Frances received the Right Livelihood Award, often called the "Alternative Nobel."

John Mackey is the chief executive officer of Whole Foods Market (www.wholefoodsmarket.com), the nation's leading purveyor of natural and organic products. Regarded by many as one of North America's most innovative—and ethical—entrepreneurs, John's fierce sense of competition, strong belief in free-market principles, staunch support for a decentralized and team-based structure, keen understanding of consumer trends, and endless supply of innovative ideas has helped build Whole Foods Market into a powerhouse. Today, more than 280 stores can be found in the United States, Canada, and the United Kingdom, all part of the mission of Whole Foods—Whole People—Whole Planet.

Moby has been making music since he was nine years old. He started out studying classical music and music theory, and then went on to play with the seminal Connecticut hardcore punk group the Vatican Commandos when he was thirteen. After leaving college he became a fixture as a dj in the late–1980s New York house and hip-hop scenes. Moby released his first single in 1990, and has since sold 20,000,000 albums. Known for his political and social activism, he has been a vegan for more than twenty years. He lives in New York City.

Danielle Nierenberg, M.S., serves as a senior researcher at the Worldwatch Institute. Her published work includes *Happier Meals: Rethinking the Global Meat Industry* (2005) and *Global Farm Animal Production and Consumption: Impacting and Mitigating Climate Change* (co-author, 2008), which was published in *Environmental Health Perspectives*, a scientific journal published by the National Institutes of Health. Her knowledge of factory farming and its global spread has been cited widely in the *New York Times Magazine*, the *International Herald Tribune*, the *Washington Post*, and other publications. Danielle worked for two years as a Peace Corps volunteer in the Dominican Republic and currently volunteers at farmers markets. She holds an M.S. in agriculture, food, and environment from Tufts University and a B.A. in environmental policy from Monmouth College.

Meredith Niles is the coordinator of the Cool Foods Campaign (www.cool foodscampaign.org), a national initiative of the CornerStone Campaign and the Center for Food Safety, a nonprofit public interest and environmental advocacy organization that challenges harmful food production technologies and promotes organic and other sustainable alternatives. Under her leadership, the Cool Foods Campaign educates consumers about the environmental impact of food choice on global warming and empowers individuals with the resources to decrease their "FoodPrint." Meredith writes extensively about agriculture, food, and climate change in a weekly guest column for Grist Environmental News and has contributed to National Public Radio, Environmental News Network, and *Political Affairs*, among other outlets.

Wayne Pacelle is the president and chief executive officer of the Humane Society of the United States (www.humanesociety.org), the nation's largest animal advocacy organization, with 11 million members and constituents; founder of Humane USA, the nonpartisan political arm of the animal protection movement; and founder of the Humane Society Legislative Fund, a 501(c)(4) social welfare organization that lobbies for animal welfare legislation and works to elect humane-minded candidates to public office. In 2007, the *New York Times* reported, "The arrival of Wayne Pacelle as head of the Humane Society in 2004 both turbocharged the farm animal welfare movement and gave it a sheen of respectability." In 2008, *Supermarket News* included Wayne on its annual Power 50 list of influential individuals in food marketing, writing that "there's no denying his growing influence on how animal agriculture is practiced in the United States."

Miyun Park serves as executive director for Global Animal Partnership (www.globalanimalpartnership.org). She has helped to bring greater interest in and policy changes for the well-being of animals raised for meat, eggs, and milk into corporate boardrooms, international investment banks, multilateral organizations, courthouses, and legislatures. Miyun has spoken on behalf of farm animals throughout the United States and in China, India, Croatia, Korea, Belgium, Egypt, and Italy, and has published dozens of articles and reports on animal agriculture and farm animal welfare, including an essay in Peter Singer's *In Defense of Animals: The Second Wave* and a chapter in *State of the Animals IV: 2007*, co-authored with Dr. Andrea Gavinelli of the European Commission. She is a board member of Farm Forward (www.farmforward.com) and serves on the editorial board of the Gateway to Farm Animal Welfare, a web portal created by the Food and Agriculture Organization of the United Nations. Before joining Global Animal Partnership, she served as vice president, Farm Animal Welfare, for the Humane Society of the United States and its global affiliate, Humane Society International.

Julie Chavez Rodriguez is currently the programs director for the Cesar E. Chavez Foundation (www.chavezfoundation.org), a nonprofit charitable organization founded in 1993 by Cesar's family and friends to educate people about his life and work and to engage all, particularly youth, to carry on his values and timeless vision for a better, more just world. Like her cousin Christine, Julie was born into the farm worker movement and learned at an early age the importance of civil rights and understood well the plight of working people. At the Foundation, Julie spearheads the educational and service programs, namely the Educating the Heart School Program and the Chavez After School Service Clubs. She is a Fellow in the National Service-Learning Emerging Leaders Initiative sponsored by the Kellogg Foundation, the National Service-Learning Partnership, and the National Youth Leadership Council. She co-authored, with Anthony Welch, the "Martin Luther King, Jr. and Cesar E. Chavez: Legacies of Leadership and Inspiration for Today's Civic Education Issue Paper," published by the Education Commission of the States in September 2005. Like her grandfather, Julie believes that "the end of all education should surely be service to others."

Paul and Phyllis Willis have dedicated their lives to promoting—and practicing—more responsible farming practices that not only benefit the welfare of animals and the integrity of the environment, but help sustain our rural communities. Paul is described by Peter Kaminsky in his book *Pig Perfect* as "among the most influential of a very few who are employing modern business practices in the service of traditional agriculture." He serves as the Manager of Niman Ranch Pork Company (www.nimanranch .com) and is the owner and operator of the Willis Free Range Pig Farm in Thornton, Iowa. Due to his expertise, he is a member of the committee convened by the National Academy of Sciences to undertake the 21st Century Systems Agriculture Project, which studies the science and policies that influence the adoption of farming practices and management systems designed to reduce the costs and environmental effects of agricultural production. Phyllis, a community activist, has hosted hundreds of guests at their farm for food and conversation, and has worked tirelessly to prevent the expansion and development of industrial factory farms.

Notes

1. Goodman J. 2009. "USDA sees a problem, not the solution," *OpEd News*, February 20. Accessed February 20, 2009.

2. Fiala N. 2008. "Meeting the demand: an estimation of potential future greenhouse gas emissions from meat production," *Ecological Economics* 67:412–9.

3. American Dietetic Association. 2007. "Position of the American Dietetic Association: food and nutrition professionals can implement practices to conserve natural resources and support ecological sustainability," *Journal of the American Dietetic Association* 107:1033–43.

4. Raskin J. 2009. "Walk, eat veggies, green your roof," *Green voice*, January 9. Accessed February 9, 2009.

5. Natural Resources Defense Council and Clean Water Network. 1998. "America's animal factories: how states fail to prevent pollution from livestock waste."

6. U.S. Environmental Protection Agency. 2003. National Pollutant Discharge Elimination System permit regulation and effluent limitation guidelines and standards for concentrated animal feeding operations (CAFOs); final rule. February 12. Federal Register 68 (29):7176, 7237.

7. "Meat: now, it's not personal!" 2004. *Worldwatch*, July/August.

8. Stull DD and Broadway MJ. 2004. *Slaughterhouse Blues: The Meat and Poultry Industry in North America* (Belmont, Calif.: Wadsworth/Thomson Learning), xiv. Foreword by Eric Schlosser.

9. Spellman FR and Whiting NE. 2007. *Environmental Management of Concentrated Animal Feeding Operations (CAFOs)* (Boca Raton, FL: Taylor & Francis Group), 6–7.

10. Purdy J. 2002. "The new culture of rural America," *The American Prospect*, November 30.

11. Rollin, BE. 1995. *Farm Animal Welfare: Social, Bioethical, and Research Issues* (Ames, Iowa: Iowa State University Press).

12. Grandin T. 2001. "Corporations can be agents of great improvements in animal welfare and food safety and the need for minimum decent standards." A paper presented at the National Institute of Animal Agriculture on April 4.

13. Tabler GT and Mendenhall AM. 2003. "Broiler nutrition, feed intake and grower economics," *Avian Advice* 5 (4):8–10.

14. Byrnes J. 1976. "Raising pigs by the calendar at Maplewood Farms," *Hog Farm Management*, September, p. 30.

15. Taylor LJ. 1978. *National Hog Farmer*, March, p. 27.

16. U.S. Department of Agriculture Food Safety and Inspection Service. 2006. *Veal from farm to table.*

17. Rajendra Pachauri, chair of the Intergovernmental Panel on Climate Change, quoted in Jowit J. 2008. "UN says eat less meat to curb global warming," *The Guardian*, September 7. Accessed January 15, 2009.

18. European Parliament Report on "2050: The future begins today— recommendations for the EU's future integrated policy on climate change," Temporary Committee on Climate Change. October 12. Accessed March 25, 2008.

19. McMichael AJ, Powles JW, Butler CD, and Uauy R. 2007. "Food, livestock production, energy, climate change, and health. The Lancet Energy and Health Series," *The Lancet* 370 (9594):1253–63.

20. Harvard School of Public Health Nutrition Source. 2009. "5 quick tips: following the Healthy Eating Pyramid," Accessed February 5, 2009.

21. "Position of the American Dietetic Association and Dietitians of Canada: vegetarian diets," 2003, *Journal of the American Dietetic Association* 103 (6):748–765.

22. "Precautionary moratorium on new concentrated animal feed operations," 2003 Policy Statements of the American Public Health Association.

23. Human Rights Watch. 2004. *Blood, Sweat, and Fear: Workers' Rights in U.S. Meat and Poultry Plants* (New York: Human Rights Watch), 24.

24. Human Rights Watch. 2004. *Blood, Sweat, and Fear: Workers' Rights in U.S. Meat and Poultry Plants* (New York: Human Rights Watch), 30–31.

25. Human Rights Watch. 2004. *Blood, Sweat, and Fear: Workers' Rights in U.S. Meat and Poultry Plants* (New York: Human Rights Watch), 33.

26. Stull DD and Broadway MJ. 2004. *Slaughterhouse Blues: The Meat and Poultry Industry in North America* (Belmont, Calif.: Wadsworth/Thomson Learning), 77.

27. Kennedy RF Jr. 2006. "Good food versus green eggs and ham," *Waterkeeper*, Spring, pp. 4–5.

28. Trom B. 2005. "Say no to factory farms: health and prosperity of rural communities at stake," *The Grand Forks Herald*, February 28.

29. "Precautionary moratorium on new concentrated animal feed operations," 2003 Policy Statements of the American Public Health Association.

30. Akhtar AZ, Greger M, Ferdowsian H, and Frank E. 2009. "Health professionals' roles in animal agriculture, climate change, and human health," *American Journal of Preventive Medicine* 36 (2):182–7.

31. International Finance Corporation. 2006. "Good practice note: animal welfare in livestock operations," October, no. 6.

32. Chu S. 2007. "The world's energy problem and what we can do about it." Talk given at University of California-Berkeley on January 31 when Chu was director of Lawrence Berkeley National Laboratory. Accessed January 26, 2009.

33. Baroni L, Cenci L, Tettamanti M, and Berati M. 2007. "Evaluating the environmental impact of various dietary patterns combined with different food production systems," *European Journal of Clinical Nutrition* 61:279–86.

Illustration Credits and Information

Page 7: **Chicken**: Johnson Jr., et al., "Antimicrobial-resistant and Extraintestinal Pathogenic Escherichia Coli in Retail Foods," *Journal of Infectious Diseases* 205 (2005), 1040–9; J.L Smith and D. Bayles, "Postinfectious Irritable Bowel Syndrome: A Long-term Consequence of Bacterial Gastroenteritis," *Journal of Food Protection* 70:7 (July 2007), 1762–9. **Fish**: P. Carta, et al., "Sub-clinical Neurobehavioral Abnormalities Associated with Low Level of Mercury Exposure Through Fish Consumption," *Neurotoxicology* 24:4–5 (2003), 617–23; J.G. Mackert Jr. and A. Berglund, "Mercury Exposure from Dental Amalgam Fillings: Absorbed Dose and the Potential for Adverse Health Effects," *Critical Review of Oral Biology and Nedicine* 8:4 (1997), 410–36. **Pork**: C.M. Degiorgio, et al., "Neurocysticercosis," *Epilepsy Currents* 4:3 (May–June 2004), 107–11. **Beef**: J. Collinge, "Variant Creutzfeldt-Jakob Disease," *Lancet* 354 (1999), 317–23; P. Brown, et al., "Infectivity Studies of Both Ash and Air Emissions from Simulated Incineration of Scrapie-contaminated Tissues," *Environmental Science and Technology* 38:22 (November 15, 2004), 6155–60. **Eggs**: C.M. Schroeder, et al., "Estimate of Illnesses from *Salmonella Enteritidis* in Eggs, United States, 2000," *Emerging Infectious Diseases* 11:1 (2005), 113–5; L. Djoussé and J.M. Gaziano, "Egg Consumption in Relation to Cardiovascular Disease and Mortality: The Physicians' Health Study," *American Journal of Clinical Nutrition* 87:4 (April 2008), 964–9; D.R. Jacobs Jr., et al., "Whole-grain Consumption Is Associated with a Reduced Risk of Noncardiovascular, Noncancer Death Attributed to Inflammatory Diseases in the Iowa Women's Health Study," *American Journal of Clinical Nutrition* 85:6 (June 2007), 1606–14; A. Ternhag, et al., "Short- and Long-term Effects of Bacterial Bastrointestinal Infections," *Emerging Infectious Diseases* 14: 1 (January 2008), 143–8. **Dairy**: C.A. Adebamowo, et al., "Milk Consumption and Acne in Teenaged Boys," *Journal of the American Academy of Dermatology* 58:5 (May 2008), 787–93; F.W. Danby, "Diet and Acne," *Clinical Dermatology*

26:1 (January–February 2008), 93–6; Q. Sun, et al., "Plasma and Erythrocyte Biomarkers of Dairy Fat Intake and Risk of Ischemic Heart Disease," *American Journal of Clinical Nutrition* 86:4 (October 2007), 929–37; van der pols jc, et al., "Childhood Dairy Intake and Adult Cancer Risk: 65-y Follow-up of the Boyd Orr Cohort, *American Journal of Clinical Nutrition* 86:6 (December 2007), 1722–9; P.N. Mitrou, et al., "A Prospective Study of Dietary Calcium, Dairy Products, and Prostate Cancer Risk (Finland)," *International Journal of Cancer* 120:11 (June 1, 2007), 2466–73; A. Stang, et al., "Adolescent Milk Fat and Galactose Consumption and Testicular Germ Cell Cancer," *Cancer Epidemiology, Biomarkers & Prevention* 15:11 (November 2006), 2189–95; H. Chen, et al., "Consumption of Dairy Products and Risk of Parkinson's Disease. *American Journal of Epidemiology* 165:9 (May 1, 2007), 998–1006.

Page 9: Compiled from data provided by the Association of American Feed Control Officials and the Food Animal Residue Avoidance Databank (FARAD).Poultry litter includes excreta, feathers, spilled feed, substrate, soil, and dead birds. J.P. Graham, et al., "Antibiotic-Resistant *Enterococci* and *Staphylococci* Isolated from Flies Collected Near Confined Poultry-feeding Operations," *Science of the Total Environment* 407:8 (2009), 2701–10.

Page 11: P. Rusin, P. Orosz-Coughlin, and C. Gerba, "Reduction of Faecal Coliform, Coliform and Heterptrophic Plate Count Bacteria in the Household Kitchen and Bathroom by Disinfection with Hypochlorite Cleaners," *Journal of Applied Microbiology* 85:5 (November 1998), 819–28.

Page 16: Compiled from data provided by the U.S. Government Accountability Office for 2008.

Page 19: R. Goldburg, et al., "Marine Aquaculture In the United States," prepared for the Pew Oceans Commission (2001); The Humane Society of the United States, "An Humane Society of the United States Report: The Welfare of Animals in Open Aquaculture Systems (2009).

Page 20: Compiled from data provided by D. Heederick, et al., "Health Effects of Airborne Exposures from Concentrated Animal Feeding Operations," *Environmental Health Perspectives* 115: 2 (2007), 298–302; The Humane Society of the United States' report "Factory Farming in America"; and the Clean Air Task Force's 2004 report "Dirty Air, Dirty Power: Mortality and Health Damage Due to Air Pollution from Power Plants."

Page 24: Calculations based on data provided by J.L. Lusk and F.B. Norwood, "Some Economic Benefits and Costs of Vegetarianism," *Agricultural and Resource Economics Review* (forthcoming, as of summer 2009).

Page 28: Data provided by the Union of Concerned Scientists, published in: D. Gurian-Sherman, "CAFOS Uncovered" (2008).

Page 31: Data compiled and provided by the Union of Concerned Scientists, published in: D. Gurian-Sherman, "CAFOS Uncovered" (2008).

Page 35: Compiled from data provided by the U.S. Government Accountability Office (GAO).

Page 36: Compiled from data provided by the U.S. Government Accountability Office (GAO).

Pages 38–44: Compiled from data provided for 2008 by the U.S. Department of Agricultureand Industry Trade Associations.

Page 57: About the digits: population figures from the U.S. Census Bureau per-capita chicken consumption from the national chicken council. Emissions facts from the U.S. Environmental Protection Agency for a typical passenger vehicle. Average pounds of carbon emissions involved in the production of one pound of chicken from the Food and Agriculture Organization of the United Nations' Livestock Longshadow. 2010 figures are projected by the U.S. Census Bureau and the National Chicken Council.

Page 68: T. Colin Campbell, PhD, professor emeritus of nutritional biochemistry at Cornell University and bestselling author of *The China Study*, describing the most comprehensive scientificstudy of health and nutrition conducted to date. C.L.Perry, et al., "Adolescent Vegetarians: How Well Do Their Dietary Patterns Meet the Healthy People 2010 Objectives?" *Archives of Pediatrics & Adolescent Medicine* 156:5 (2002), 431–7.

Page 74: ***Tuna Fish***: L. Trasande, et al., "Public Health and Economic Consequences of Methyl Mercury Toxicity to the Developing Brain," *Environmental Health Perspectives* 113:5 (2005), 590–6; P. Carta, et al., "Sub-clinical Neurobehavioral Abnormalities Associated with Low Level of Mercury Exposure Through Fish Consumption," *Neurotoxicology* 24:4–5 (2003), 617–23; FDA, "Thimerosal in Vaccines," 2009. ***Eggs:*** F. Courant, et

al. "Exposure Assessment of Prepubertal Children to Steroid Endocrine Disruptors. 2. Determination of Steroid Hormones in Milk, Egg, and Meat Samples," *Journal of Agricultural and Food Chemistry* 56:9 (2008), 3176–84; D. Maume, et al., "Assessment of Estradiol and Its Metabolites in Meat," *Acta Pathologica et Microbiologica Scandinavica* 109:1 (2001), 32–8. **Hotdogs**: S. Sarasua and D.A. Savitz, "Cured and Broiled Meat Consumption in Relation to Childhood Cancer: Denver, Colorado (United States)," *Cancer Causes and Control* 5:2 (1994), 141–8; J.M. Peters, et al., "Processed Meats and Risk of Childhood Leukemia (California, USA)," *Cancer Causes and Control* 5:2 (1994), 195–202. **Chicken "fingers"**: A. Schechter and L. Li, "Dioxins, Dibenzofurans, Dioxin-like PCBs, and DDE in U.S. Fast Food, 1995" *Chemosphere* 35:5–7 (1997), 1449–57.

Page 80: Iowa State University Extension, "Livestock Confinement Dust and Gases: Table 2."

Page 84: Compiled by data provided by the U.S. Bureau of Labor Statistics for 2007. *According to Human Rights Watch, the federal agency "OSHA [Occupational Safety and Health Administration] administrators and independent researchers have found a common corporate practice of underreporting injuries of all kinds . . . as high as 69 percent . . . according to OSHA, the reported data from the Bureau of Labor Statistics (BLS): seriously understate the true risk . . . many peer-reviewed studies have been published in the scientific literature in the last 18 years that document . . . extensive and widespread underreporting on the OSHA log of occupational injuries and illnesses. . . ." As such, it is important to note that these statistics likely significantly underscore the true rate of injury.

Page 92: P. Korsching, et al., "Iowa Farm and Rural life Poll: 2003 Summary Report," Iowa State University Extension (2004).

Page 96: (1) K. Thu, et al., "A Control Study of the Physical and Mental Health of Residents Living Near a Large-scale Swine Operation," *Journal of Agricultural Safety and Health* 3:1 (1997), 13–26; (2) S. Sneeringer, "Does Animal Feeding Operation Pollution Hurt Public Health? A National Longitudinal Study of Health Externalities Identified by Geographic Shifts In Livestock Production," *American Journal of Agricultural Economics* 91:1 (2009), 124–37; (3) S.S. Schiffman, et al., "The Effect of Environmental Odors Emanating from Commercial Swine Operations on the Mood of Nearby

Residents," *Brain Research Bulletin* 37:4 (1995), 369–75; (4) S. Wing and S. Wolf, "Intensive Livestock Operations, Health, and Quality of Life Among Eastern North Carolina Residents," *Environmental Health Perspectives* 108:3 (2000), 233–8; (5) J.A. Merchant, et al., "Asthma and Farm Exposures in a Cohort of Rural Iowa Children," *Environmental Health Perspectives* 113:3 (2005), 350–6.

Page 99: C. Stofferahn, "Industrialized Farming and Its Relationship to Community Well-being," an update of a 2000 report by Linda Lobao, prepared for the State of North Dakota, office of the attorney general, W. Weida, 2004, considering the rationales for factory farming (2006).

Page 104: M. Greger, "The Human/Animal Interface: Emergence and Resurgence of Zoonotic Infectious Dieases," *Critical Reviews in Microbiology* 33 (2007), 243–99.

Page 108: Excerpted from the U.S. Centers for Disease Control and Prevention's "foodborne illness" > "frequently asked questions" online resource (http://www.cdc.gov/ncidod/dbmd/diseaseinfo/foodborneinfections_g.htm).

Page 109: U.S. Department of the Interior, U.S. Geological Survey.

Page 114: Based on data from "Water: More Nutrition Per Drop," by the Stockholm International Water Institute and the International Water Mangement Institute.

Page 116: V. Smil, *Enriching the Earth: Fritz Haber, Carl Bosch, and the Transformation of World Food Production* (Cambridge: MIT Press, 2004).

Page 121: E. Millstone and T. Lang, *The Penguin Atlas of Food* (London: Penguin Books, 2003).